From The Guys Who Were There...
The Kansas City Royals

with

**George Brett • Eric Hosmer
Salvador Perez • Lorenzo Cain
Mike Moustakas • Alex Gordon
Mike Sweeney • and more!**
by Bill Althaus

Foreword by Denny Matthews

ASCEND BOOKS

"It was funny, the other day I was sitting in the stands in the Rogers Centre (in Toronto) and the Blue Jays are beating us and (about to force) a Game 6 back in Kansas City and I'm thinking to myself, 'What if they do the same thing to us that we did to them in 1985?' **George Brett**

Major League Baseball Hall of Fame

Royals Hall of Fame

Kansas City Royals Vice President

"When you're playing, every game is so important. But you have to take time to enjoy it, savor every moment. And that's what I like about this Royals team. They are enjoying every moment and sharing the experience with their fans." **Buddy Biancalana**

Kansas City Royals shortstop, 1982-1987

World Series champion

"Does life get any better than this? No. It doesn't get any better than winning a World Series, it really doesn't. Now, the rest of the guys on this year's team get to experience that feeling." **Frank White**

Kansas City Royals second baseman, 1973-1990

Royals Hall of Fame

Five-time All-Star

Eight-time Gold Glove Award winner

"I mean, we're a tight-knit group here. We all get along. I know we always say we have good chemistry. But we really do. We're all pulling for each other. We all get along off the field. And sometimes that's not always the case. I've been on teams where some guys don't get along with other people. Over the past few years that has changed. Maybe it's the leadership in here, the guys Dayton's brought in here; but everyone gets along really well. Everyone's fighting for the same thing, and that's winning games every day." **Alex Gordon**

Kansas City Royals left fielder

Three-time All-Star

Four-time Gold Glove Award winner

"I think we never panic, and the reason why we are so laid back it seems like to everybody, is because we are believers that this group of guys in here can, over the course of 162 games, be elite."   **Eric Hosmer**
Kansas City Royals first baseman
Three-time Gold Glove Award winner

"Being around here for the last six years, we feel comfortable you know. We feel like a family here. And you know, the best thing I can do on the team, I like to do, is make my teammates happy. You know, be happy. Enjoy the game. Play hard. But have fun, too. It's a game, you know?"   **Salvador Perez**
Kansas City Royals catcher
Three-time All-Star
2015 World Series MVP
Three-time Gold Glove Award winner

"The parade – our fans gave us the greatest gift they could give us and that is this turnout and a lifelong memory. I want to come back (and manage next year). I love being here and I feel like we are in a position where we can keep on winning."   **Ned Yost**
Kansas City Royals manager

"There's not a bad dude in this clubhouse. We just pull for each other. We're like brothers on a Little League team. You're playing for a whole lot, but you're playing for each other more than you're playing for yourself and I think that's the biggest part of why we have done so well."   **Danny Duffy**
Kansas City Royals pitcher

"Like many men, showing emotions isn't a strong suit of mine, but as I got home that night of the (2014) Wild Card game I tried take in all that happened. I just kept playing back the night and couldn't believe it – I actually started to cry."   **Cody Thorn**
Lifelong Royals Fan

Requests for permission should be addressed to: Ascend Books, LLC, Attn: Rights and Permissions Department, 12710 Pflumm Road, Suite 200, Olathe, KS. 66062

10 9 8 7 6 5 4 3 2 1

ISBN: (print) 978-0-9966742-0-1
ISBN: (e-book) 978-0-9966742-1-8
Library of Congress Control Number: 2015957469

Publisher: Bob Snodgrass
Managing Editor: Aaron Cedeño
Publication Coordinator: Christine Drummond
Sales and Marketing: Lenny Cohen and Sandy Hipsh
Dust Jacket and Book Design: Rob Peters

All photos courtesy of Bill Althaus unless otherwise indicated.

Every reasonable attempt has been made to determine the ownership of copyright. This book is not an official publication, and as such is not affiliated with, endorsed, or licensed by Major League Baseball or the Kansas City Royals.

Please notify the publisher of any erroneous credits or omissions, and corrections will be made to subsequent editions/future printings.

The goal of Ascend Books is to publish quality works. With that goal in mind, we are proud to offer this book to our readers. Please note, however, that the story, experiences, and the words are those of the authors alone.

Printed in the United States of America

www.ascendbooks.com

Table of Contents

Dedication

This book is dedicated to Royals fans everywhere. We've waited a long time to see the crown of Major League Baseball returned home. And now the rest of the world knows what we've known all along:

Kansas City isn't just the City of Fountains. It's the City of Champions.

Bill Althaus

Foreword

I wasn't surprised.

By now, don't we all pretty much expect perfection from Wade Davis? The guy has had two essentially flawless seasons out of the Kansas City bullpen. When he comes in, it's pretty much a done deal. So when he blew the final pitch of the 2015 season past the Mets' Wilmer Flores, sure it was big. It was huge. Everyone knows the story, that for the first time in three decades the Royals were World Series champions.

It just wasn't surprising, that's all. It wasn't a shock, and for more reasons than the fact that Wade Davis was on the mound.

I don't think it's uncommon to take a minute to reflect during moments such as that, and my thoughts couldn't help but drift to last year, when they came up 90-feet short of tying Game 7 of the World Series. That became motivation for 2015. You can go back to Spring Training, which doesn't mean anything – it's just preparation for the season – but that was the mindset. This team set out from the very first pitch of Spring Training with the image of Alex Gordon standing on third base burned into their brains. They were betting they were 90-feet better than last year. And they were right.

I think one of the silliest things people do – and I understand why they do it, because I do it, too – is read pre-season magazines and all their predictions. Number one, who is going to be hurt, and for how long? What if it's one of your best players? That's impossible to predict. Who predicted Alex Gordon would be out for six weeks? Nobody. How good are the teams in the division going to be? Are they going to be better, worse, or the same? There are so many things that factor in.

But the one constant the Royals kept with them was the motivation provided by those 90-feet. It carried them right through Spring Training, and into the season with such a hot start, and really it never let up. They got off to a great start, and just to be honest about it, it was pretty much a free ride through our division. The Royals were never pressured. The one team with the possibility to challenge was Minnesota, but we played a three-game series up there, and I think I even said this on the air, but they were so young. The Royals were more experienced, more athletic, and simply a better team.

Luck is so much a part of the game of baseball, and the Royals have benefited greatly the past two seasons from a lot of good fortune. I think everyone would admit that. But there's another side to having things break your way – you have to have the players to take advantage of it. And if you don't, that good fortune can turn on you just as quickly. I'm also a big believer in 'It's your turn.' The losing seasons weren't going to last forever. At some point, the Royals were going to get the right combination of players and coaches and front office staff to make the club successful again. It wasn't their turn for 30 years, but I think if you go back five years or so, and you see the drafting and the players coming up through the system, you could see things starting to shift. There were players with very good physical ability who enjoyed the game, worked hard, wanted to get better, and were winners all through the minor league system. The only question, then: How would they adapt to the big leagues? How much would they improve at the Major League level? And would they be winners in Kansas City as they were in the minor leagues?

Photo Courtesy Bob Snodgrass

Kendrys Morales takes a hack at a pitch during spring training in April 2015, while Salvador Perez watches from the on-deck circle. Morales was one of a handful of Royals acquired during the off-season by general manager Dayton Moore who ended up paying massive dividends for the club during the 2015 season.

If you take a look back at the best teams in Royals history, this one reminds me most closely of the 1977 team. I know the 1985 boys won the World Series, but for my money that '77 group is still the best; still the only Royals team to win 100 games. Now compare them to the 2015 Royals. The biggest difference is probably starting pitching versus bullpen. '77 had the better rotation, '15 had the better bullpen. But everywhere else they align so closely. Offense was similar, defense was similar – with the caveat that while both teams made the plays you expected them to make, I think this year's team had a little more of a flair for the dramatic. They made the spectacular play more often.

They were similar in what they did for the people of Kansas City and the surrounding area as well. It was electric. In '77, you'd walk the parking lot after a game and see license plates from six or seven different states. People were coming from all over. It was the same thing this year. There was a solid fanbase waiting amid the losing seasons. You knew once they were contenders again, the fans would be back in force. And there are more people here in Kansas City now than there were then. There wasn't any doubt in my mind they would come back and be there just like they were in the halcyon days. And just look at the attendance figures. Look at the crowd that showed up for the parade. That's all the proof you need.

It was a terrific season, and one long in the making. And now I get asked 'Can we do it again?' I don't know. It's harder now than it was 30 years ago, because there are more playoff teams, and a lot of times the Wild Card winner is in a better spot than the divisional champions. Just look at the 2014 World Series. Both Wild Card teams!

Winning depends on so many things – the injuries, the breaks. What's their motivation? Those 90-feet are used up. That tank is dry. So what's your mindset to get better? Are you satisfied with 2015? Is that the end of the show, or is there an encore waiting in the wings? Who knows? Nobody knows.

Can we do it again? I can't answer that. But, boy, it would sure be fun.

Denny Matthews
Royals Hall of Fame – Class of 2004
Ford C. Frick Award Recipient – National Baseball Hall of Fame – 2007

INTRODUCTION

A 29-Year Retrospective

It was going to take more than a broken leg to keep me away from the Kansas City Royals' season opener back in 1969.

It was the biggest day of my young life; the first-ever game in the history of a club that would eventually bring Kansas City a pair of world championships and a lifetime of memories. It would bring us players like George Brett, Frank White, Eric Hosmer, Lorenzo Cain, Alex Gordon and Salvador Perez.

Charlie Finley took my beloved Kansas City A's to Oakland in 1967, and I didn't have a team to watch in 1968.

My mom and dad bought me a radio – a really, really big radio – that I swore could pick up signals from outer space, and I was able to listen to baseball broadcasts from across the country.

I even listened to Catfish Hunter throw a no-hitter against the Minnesota Twins. That was a bittersweet moment for a 15-year-old, as Catfish was my favorite player when he was a youngster with the A's.

But thanks to Sen. Stuart Symington and Ewing Kauffman, baseball returned to Kansas City in 1969 and I had a great seat a few rows back from the visitor's dugout at old Municipal Stadium.

My mom was my chauffeur, and I can't even begin to tell you how many times she drove me from Independence to 22nd and Brooklyn to drop me off for a game. On this day, she stayed and watched the Royals edge the Twins 4-3 in 12 innings.

Moe Drabowsky, a flaky reliever who would often put goldfish in the water cooler of the visitor's bullpen, won the game. Joe Keough drove in Joe Foy with the winning run.

A kid named Lou Piniella, who would go on to win the American League Rookie of the Year Award and later become a World Series-winning manager with the Cincinnati Reds, had four hits for the Royals.

The win was thrilling, but the most special moment of the day came before the game even started. I was on crutches with a cast that extended from my right ankle to my hip, courtesy of a freak wrestling injury I suffered my seventh-grade year at Palmer Junior High School.

I was hobbling to the bathroom near the left field concession stands when a voice from the field called out, "Hey kid, what happened to your leg?"

It was Piniella, who was playing catch with Jerry Adair.

I told him I broke it wrestling and he said, "Here, maybe this will make you feel better."

He then tossed me a baseball. I snagged it, and I suddenly had a new baseball hero.

During the past four decades, I have had more baseball heroes than I could describe in the space provided for this chapter, but "Sweet Lou" will always rank among my favorites.

While heroes were in short supply for the Royals during the lean years following their 1985 World Series victory, their 2014 edition created a whole new gallery of players worthy of wearing a T-shirt with their name emblazoned across the back – Hosmer, Moose, Perez and Ventura.

Every Royals game is special, but there is something extra special about the magic that comes on Opening Day.

I can recall every hit, pitch, fielding gem and magical moment like it happened only yesterday.

I won't be on crutches, and I'll have 46 home openers under my belt, but I'll still feel like that 15-year-old kid who caught a ball from Lou Piniella before watching the start of a new baseball era in Kansas City.

SUNNY OUTLOOK

April 6, 2015. The skies were gloomy and overcast, but inside Kauffman Stadium it was all smiles, as the defending American League champion

Kansas City Royals roughed up the Chicago White Sox 10-1 to claim their first Opening Day win in six seasons.

A lengthy pregame ceremony, in which every member of the Royals organization received a 2014 American League championship ring, did not faze starter Yordano Ventura, who at 23 years old became the team's youngest Opening Day starter since Steve Busby took the mound 42 years ago.

Ventura had it dialed in on cruise control through six innings, allowing just two hits and no runs.

Chicago's Jose Abreu lined a home run into the left field bleachers with one out in the seventh and cleanup hitter Adam LaRoche fouled off a pitch before Ventura jumped off the mound in obvious pain as he grabbed the thumb on his right (pitching) hand.

Manager Ned Yost and the team's training staff ran to the mound as Ventura rolled around in pain.

"I was running over to second and looked out at the mound and saw 'Ace' rolling around on the ground and thought, 'Oh my gosh, what happened?'" said third baseman Mike Moustakas, who had a homer, single and sacrifice bunt from his new No. 2 spot in the lineup.

"It looked like he was hurting pretty good, and none of us knew what happened, especially since the ball was fouled off. It looked like he'd been hit, or something."

The Royals announced later that Ventura experienced a cramp in his thumb and that the injury was not serious.

"He gets them all the time," Yost said in his postgame news conference. "When I saw it I figured he was cramping up, it was just worse than it usually is. Before that, everything was working for him. It was a good way to start the season – except for the cramp."

Later, Ventura addressed the media and talked about his Opening Day start through interpreter and teammate Jeremy Guthrie.

"I felt it lock up on me," Ventura said. "I thought at first it was something really bad. I'm happy that it isn't, and I'm not concerned about missing any time with what happened. Just a cramp that surprised me, but I feel confident going forward.

"I have had them before, but never as serious as today. I've pitched through them without letting anybody know that I had them. This one was different."

Ventura gave up one run through six-plus innings and got the victory.

The lanky youngster, who just signed a five-year deal with the Royals, made his debut in the national spotlight in the 2014 World Series, throwing seven scoreless innings in a 10-0 Game 6 win.

Little did we know that our boys in blue were about to make a repeat attempt to bring the Crown home, and what a journey it would be.

Bill Althaus

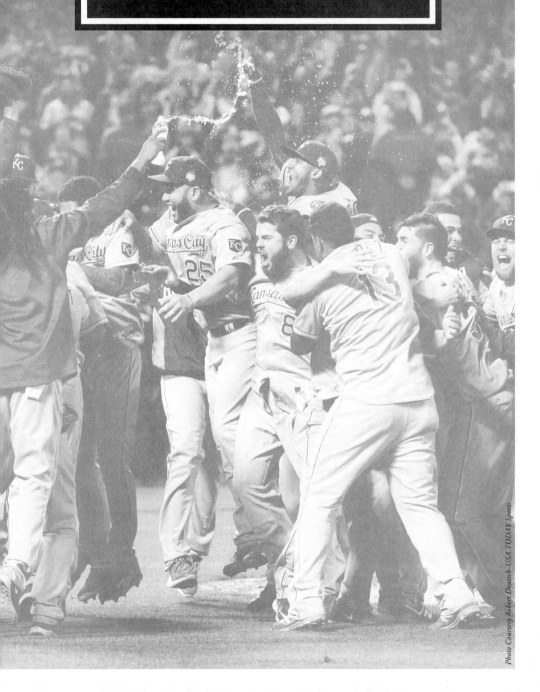

The Legends

CHAPTER 1

Number 5 Passes the Torch

Salvador Perez was not even born the last time the Kansas City Royals won a World Series, yet when asked about the 1985 championship season and what he knew about that team he simply smiled and said, "George Brett was on that team. George Brett was the man."

Ask anyone who follows the game, and they will tell you the Hall of Fame third baseman turned in the greatest performance of his storied

Photo Courtesy Peter G. Aiken-USA TODAY Sports

Oct 14, 2015; Kansas City, MO, USA; Kansas City Royals Hall of Fame player George Brett (left) talks with Royals left fielder Alex Gordon (right) prior to Game 5 of the ALDS against the Houston Astros at Kauffman Stadium. Brett was a cornerstone of the Royals' last World Series champion club back in 1985, and has remained an active partner in the organization as a vice president.

career in Game 3 of the American League Championship Series - against the same Toronto team the Royals topped in six thrilling games in the 2015 ALCS.

The Kansas City icon was 4-for-4 with four runs scored, two home runs and three RBI. His team was down two games to none and would eventually come back from a three games to one deficit to top the Blue Jays and the National League champion St. Louis Cardinals.

"I had a game where I hit for the cycle, with two homers, against Baltimore, but no one remembers that game because it wasn't in the playoffs," said Brett, who is a vice president in the Royals front office.

"It was funny, the other day I was sitting in the stands in the Rogers Centre (in Toronto) and the Blue Jays are beating us and forcing a Game 6 back in Kansas City and I'm thinking to myself, 'What if they do the same thing to us that we did to them in 1985?'

"We all know it didn't happen because (Lorenzo) Cain scores from first on (Eric) Hosmer's single and then Wade Davis – man, that Wade Davis! – comes out and gets out of jam (runners on second and third and no outs) in the top of the ninth to get a 4-3 win.

"I thought I was going to have a heart attack. I mean it, a freaking heart attack. It's so much different when you're not playing and just watching. Although I'll tell you something – when they had the runners on second and third and two outs and (Josh) Donaldson at the plate, I'd have been thinking, 'Oh God, hit it to anyone but me.' And he hits the ground ball to Moose (Mike Moustakas) at third base and we win.

"I was never so happy or relieved in my life."

And he was never better than that chilly night, Oct. 11, 1985, at Royals Stadium.

"George said, 'Climb on my back boys,' and we did," pitcher Mark Gubicza recalled. "He was the guy you wanted at the plate in the biggest moments of the game. Man it was fun watching him play."

Willie Wilson singled in the bottom of the first but was thrown out in an unsuccessful steal attempt.

"With Willie on first, I'm thinking fastball," Brett said. "When he was thrown out, I'm thinking changeup."

A changeup is exactly what he got from starter Doyle Alexander and Brett hit a home run to deep right field to make it a 1-0 game. He thought he had his second homer of the night with his very next at bat, but the ball caromed off the top of the outfield wall and he had to settle for a double.

"I always pride myself on running out every ball I hit, but I thought that was a (bleeping) homer and I didn't run as hard," Brett said. "I should have been at third and there I was at second."

But he would eventually score, as Hal McRae hit a fly ball to send Brett to third and he scored on Frank White's sacrifice fly to make it 2-0.

The Jays responded with five runs in the fifth, and took a 5-3 lead into the sixth when Brett managed to launch his second big fly of the night into the seats.

He led off the eighth inning of a 5-5 game and hit a single. He scored the game winning run on a blooper by Steve Balboni and the Royals were on their way to one of the most memorable stretches in postseason history.

"The guys this year are capable of winning it all," Brett said, in the immediate aftermath of clinching back-to-back World Series berths.

He didn't yet know he'd soon be able to add "baseball prophet" to his resume.

CHAPTER 2

Late Night with Buddy Biancalana

Buddy Biancalana still looks like he could put on a Kansas City Royals uniform and go out and play shortstop.

"I'm probably a better hitter now than when I played with the Royals," said Biancalana. Now 55-years-young, the former first-round draft pick is the co-founder of PMPM Sports Zone Training, located in Scottsdale, Ariz.

"If I'd have known back when I was playing what I know today about all the things that contribute to success in the field of play, well . . ."

Well, he might not have been the star of one of the most talked about segments in the history of "Late Night with David Letterman."

"It was all pretty interesting," Biancalana said, when he attended a 30th anniversary celebration of the Royals' 1985 World Series championship. "It couldn't have gone better for me, or for him."

Biancalana was hardly a candidate to share the stage with Letterman when the 1985 season started. He was a career .199 hitter who was known for his glove work at shortstop and not his batting prowess.

That same season, Cincinnati's Pete Rose was closing in on Ty Cobb's all-time hit mark of 4,121. Rose had 4,097 hits and was a sure bet to claim the crown.

Letterman, the man who turned late-night television on its head and found a way to poke fun at everything and everyone, introduced the "Buddy Biancalana Hit Countdown" in August of that memorable season. It featured likenesses of Rose and Biancalana and the number of hits they needed to pass Cobb.

"I didn't even know about it until I got calls from sportswriters who had seen the bit and wanted to know what I thought," Biancalana said.

"I thought it was funny. I wasn't getting any attention for the way I was playing, but I was sure getting a lot of it for the countdown thing."

That changed when he starred in the Royals' World Series win over the St. Louis Cardinals.

Through Game 6, when the Royals won in the bottom of the ninth to keep the series alive, Biancalana was hitting .333 with two RBIs. He finished with a .278 average and a ring.

It wasn't long after he received a call from Letterman's people. They wanted him to make an appearance on the show.

"I was surprised," Biancalana admitted. "And couldn't wait to see what it would be like to be on Dave's show. We all want to be entertained in life, and if I can help entertain people a little bit, that's the sports industry. An athlete is an entertainer, as is a late-night talk show host."

Biancalana, who can hold his own with anyone in the quips department, was eager to verbally spar with the Late Night host. But that changed when he met Letterman.

"He was reserved and really shy," Biancalana said. "Which I don't think is unusual for a star like that; they have their stage personality and their real-life personality."

So Biancalana saved his hits for the field. His Royals never returned to baseball's biggest stage and Biancalana was never asked back to the Letterman show.

"But I've got some great memories – and the hit countdown clock," Biancalana said, grinning. "I don't know where it is, but I've got it somewhere."

On the other hand, he knows exactly where his World Series ring is.

"The World Series is something special, and it's so great that the fans in Kansas City are experiencing that again," Biancalana said.

"When you're playing, every game is so important. But you have to take time to enjoy it, savor every moment. And that's what I like about this Royals team. They are enjoying every moment and sharing the experience with their fans."

CHAPTER 3

"My, oh My – Me and Jackie Robinson!"

Frank White was in his element.

The Kansas City Royals Hall of Famer was talking about his love of the team, the excitement coursing through his hometown at the very mention of the Royals, and making everyone at the Negro Leagues Baseball Museum feel special. He spent time with every fan who wanted a signature, photo, or just a few seconds to chat and relive the memories of the team's glory years.

He had just completed a Q&A session with former teammates Danny Jackson – the winner of Game 5 in both the 1985 ALCS and World Series – and fellow Royals Hall of Famer Willie Wilson, and seemed to be enjoying himself as much as the throng who waited patiently to meet the hometown hero.

Amid the amiable tumult, the legendary second-baseman took a few moments to reflect on what makes today's iteration of the Kansas City Royals so special.

"The kids on this team are having so much

Kansas City Royals Hall of Fame second baseman Frank White (right) visits with former Blue Springs South High School baseball coach Richard Wood following a Q&A session at the Negro Leagues Baseball Museum during the 2014 World Series celebration.

fun," White said. "And it's infectious. They're having so much fun, and they are sharing their wins with everyone in Kansas City. It kind of makes me jealous. I wish we would have done more for the city when we won back in 1985. Everyone is talking about this team. And I'm not just talking about Kansas City. Everyone across the country is talking about the Royals. And that's great!"

White, who won eight Gold Gloves and redefined the defensive standard at second base during the turf era, has been a player, coach, minor league manager and broadcaster for the Royals. He was relieved of his broadcasting duties in 2011.

"Now, I'm just a fan and I'm having as much fun as anyone," said White. "This is a time to celebrate what this group of players is doing to bring back the memories of the glory years and to energize a city."

In 2014, Kansas City experienced the national spotlight that comes with postseason play for the first time in 29 years, and several of the players on the roster worked with White during his stint as manager of the club's AA minor league club – then based in Wichita, Kan.

They praised White for helping advance their careers, and preparing them for the game's biggest stage.

"I really enjoyed working with Frank in the minors," four-time Gold Glove winner Alex Gordon said. "I loved him as a manager in Double-A and loved him as an announcer. It would be great to see him back on the field for the Royals some day. I'd love it and so would the other guys."

Designated hitter Billy Butler, who signed with Oakland following the 2014 season, also worked with White at the Double-A level, and shared Gordon's sentiment.

"He's a part of the history of the Royals. I loved playing for him in Wichita. He knows the game and he knew how to treat his players. He treated everyone with respect – his coaches, his players and the fans. The fans loved him. Everyone loved Frank. It would be great to have him back. The city would embrace his return and this place would go nuts if he walked out on the field."

"It's great to just go out and enjoy a game – and you have to enjoy these games because they have all been so exciting," White said. "I love visiting with the fans, and some of them seem a little surprised when they see me in the stands.

"But it's great to be out with the fans, enjoying it just like they do. I will always be a fan of this team – always."

When he was a struggling kid trying to make a name for himself at the Kansas City Royals Baseball Academy, late owner Ewing Kauffman got him a job as a construction worker on then-Royals Stadium. He did back-breaking concrete work on the ground floor level, never dreaming that one day he would have a statue in center field alongside those of the late Dick Howser and Hall of Famer George Brett.

"It's been an amazing run," White said, who is also a county legislator for a territory that covers the area of Kansas City where he spent his childhood. "I've never been happier. I'm going to enjoy every minute of it along with all our fans."

It would be impossible to visit with the Royals legend and not talk about his memorable 1985 World Series performance, where he became the first second baseman since Jackie Robinson, the iconic Brooklyn Dodgers second baseman who broke baseball's color barrier, to hit cleanup for his team.

"My, oh my," White said, with a sense of awe in his voice. "Me and Jackie Robinson…

"When I was a kid growing up in the inner city of Kansas City, I remember playing baseball every day. When the sun came up, I made sure I had my chores done for the day and it was off to the neighborhood baseball diamond. If you couldn't find enough guys to play a game, you either improvised, or you stayed home and hit rocks with a broomstick in the driveway. I was only 7 or 8, but I'd already hit more game-winning World Series home runs than any big leaguer. My friends and I would pick the most colorful baseball names we could think of and play until our moms called us home for dinner. I was usually Diamond Jim Gentile – is that the greatest baseball name ever? The year he played for the Kansas City A's, we all wanted to be Diamond Jim. But there were other colorful names, too – Willie (Mays), The Mick (Mickey Mantle) and Johnny Callison. Doesn't that just sound like the name of a baseball player? I dreamed about being a big leaguer some day, but I never dreamed about hitting cleanup in a World Series. But it happened – thanks to Dick Howser – and I knew from the moment he called me into his office to talk about it that I wasn't going to let him down."

He had the confidence of his manager, but deep down the greatest defensive second baseman of his generation wondered if he could get the job done at the crucial Number Four spot in the order.

"That year, the World Series didn't have a designated hitter," White explained. "So Hal McRae, our designated hitter and cleanup man, wasn't able to make a big impact. Before the series started, I got to the ballpark for a practice and Dick Howser called me into the office and talked to me about his lineup. He said, 'We can't use the DH, and since you had those 22 home runs during the season and have hit fourth a few times, I'd like you to hit cleanup.'

"My eyes got real big and my mouth dropped open, and I know I kind of gave him that 'You have to be kidding me' look. I was stunned, I couldn't believe it. I was Dick's choice to hit cleanup in a World Series that all the experts had already predicted the Cardinals would win. There was a lot of pressure on Dick, and I said, 'You gotta be kidding me.' He wasn't. He just looked at me and said, 'No, I'm serious. I want you to bat cleanup.'

"When he said that, all kinds of thoughts ran through my mind. I thought, 'Why don't we let George bat fourth,' because I'm thinking about all the times the Cardinals will walk George in key situations if I'm not hitting well. What if we leave men on base because of me? George was used to hitting third and Dick wanted to keep him there. I was like, 'Okay, I'll do it. If we do well, they can write about your good decision. If we don't, they can write about how I shouldn't have been there in the first place.'

"I made a commitment to Dick, and he made a big commitment to me. I was not going to let him down. I'd had a pretty good power year with 22 homers, and he had confidence in me, which gave me confidence. I didn't want to panic. I was just wondering what the guys on the team would think."

One guy thought it was a great choice – clubhouse leader McRae, who quipped the famous line when the Cardinals led the World Series three games to one, "We got those SOBs right where we want them." That was McRae – the brash confidence and clubhouse soul of a team that had the ultimate leader on the field in Brett.

"It was the logical choice," said McRae, who immediately threw his support to his longtime friend and teammate. "Frank was such a great second baseman that people forget how good of a hitter he became late in his career. He was a great choice to hit cleanup, and he got the job done."

Though he had the blessing and support of his manager and his teammates, the national media was…less forgiving. Some outright questioned Howser's sanity, when arguably the best hitter in the game was sitting in his lineup one spot away. But White accepted the challenge and quietly promised himself that he was going to make the legacy of Jackie Robinson and Royals fans proud.

"No matter what happened, I was going to have fun with it," White said, with enthusiasm and confidence. "Then, I found out that the only other second baseman in World Series history to hit cleanup was Jackie Robinson. Just having my name mentioned in the same sentence with Jackie Robinson was inspiring and intimidating. I wasn't going to go into the series trying to be a typical cleanup hitter – I was going to do what the situation called for. If we needed to move up a runner or lay down a bunt, I was going to do it. I wasn't going to put any extra pressure on myself, and it all worked out, but all I could see was (former Kansas City Royals manager) Whitey (Herzog, who was managing the Cardinals) walking George all the time to get to me.

"Well, Game 1 rolls around and we lose 3-1. John Tudor, who was probably the best pitcher in the National League that year, shut us down. I know people looked at our lineup and thought, 'What's Frank White doing hitting cleanup?' And after we lost 3-1 and didn't generate much offense, I'm sure they were asking Dick the same thing. But Dick had more confidence in me than I might have had in myself. Back in 1983 he moved me to the third spot in the order when George got hurt, and I went on to win the Player of the Year Award, so it wasn't like I was afraid I couldn't do that job. I didn't have any problems hitting fourth; I didn't have any problems facing Tudor or any of their other pitchers. I just kept thinking that this is the World Series and I've only got one shot to hit fourth and I wanted to make the most of it. I wanted to make a difference. I wanted to reward Dick for having that much confidence in me."

But the questions from the media were relentless. After they grilled Howser, they cornered White at his locker. He showed the same grace and poise answering the questions as he did at the plate and in the field.

"After that first game, reporters were asking me about hitting cleanup and about the Cardinals being such heavy favorites," White said. "And I told them I didn't know why they were such heavy favorites. We had hit more home runs, I thought we were as fast as they were and even though our pitching staff was young, I thought we were as good as they were and we had (reliever Dan) Quisenberry, who was the best closer in the game. In a short series, that first game is so important, and we had just come off that crazy series with the Blue Jays so there wasn't any panic in our locker room.

"I think we were a reflection of Dick – he was calm and so were we. Dick wasn't the kind of guy to panic, he was a Yankee guy, he knew how to handle veteran guys, he knew how to handle pressure, so he didn't panic and I think that was the most important thing for us. We'd lost the first game at home, but we knew there were six games left in the series. Once we lost Game 1, it was okay, that's gone, let's focus on Game 2. Don't think too far ahead. And then we lose Game 2, and it wasn't just that we lost it, we lost it 4-2 when St. Louis scored four runs in the top of the ninth inning. It was a well-played game and we led 2-0 going into the ninth, so it wasn't like we were getting blown out. We lost two very close games, and were looking forward to taking the series to St. Louis and trying to find a way to get a win."

And that's when the Royals' charter flight landed at Lambert Airport in St. Louis and saw a banner that helped change the course of World Series history. It read:

WELCOME TO ST. LOUIS, THE HOME OF
THE 1985 WORLD CHAMPIONS

It goes without saying that the infamous banner lit a fire under White and his teammates that was finally extinguished by a joyous champagne celebration following an 11-0 win in Game 7.

"After we lost Game 2 at home, the mood was surprisingly upbeat," White explained. "We'd been down 3-1 to Toronto so we knew we had the ability to come back in a short series. All we needed was a win – and when we landed in St. Louis, we got all the motivation we needed. When we got off the plane, we saw this large banner that said: WELCOME TO ST. LOUIS, THE HOME OF THE 1985 WORLD SERIES CHAMPIONS. If that doesn't motivate you, nothing will.

"You know that old saying, 'It's never over 'til it's over.' Well, that's how we felt. You could just see the mood change in all the guys when we saw that sign – and there were signs everywhere. Thank you, St. Louis, for all the motivation. And we all knew that the real motivating factor was having Sabes (Cy Young Award winner Bret Saberhagen) on the mound for Game 3. I'd gone hitless in Game 1, and had three hits and an RBI in Game 2, but we lost, so I was hoping to have a breakout game in Game 3. And I did. We got a couple of runs in the fourth inning and we all felt like those were all the runs we'd need. Then I hit a two-run homer off (Joaquin) Andujar in the fifth, making it 4-0 and we're thinking, 'Bring 'em on for Game 4.'

"That was the longest home run I ever hit – and the most special. When I hit it, I watched (Tito) Landrum in left field and he never moved. When you're not known for hitting home runs, and you get one like that you're always going to remember it. I knew it was gone, so I wanted to make sure I ran the bases just right – not too fast and not too slow. I tried to be the ultimate professional and not show up the other team or the other pitcher. I still get chill bumps just thinking about it. I'd hit that home run a thousand times in the alley behind my house and in the park in our neighborhood, but now it really happened. I just wish I had that bat. It was one of (catcher) Jim Sundberg's bats and I shaved down the handle and it was just perfect.

"With Sabes pitching, you knew you were going to win – and we did, 6-1. He was 20 and was so skinny, and he was trying to grow that little mustache of his. I bet he celebrated that night, but I was so exhausted I just went back to the hotel to rest up for the next game. There were a lot of Royals fans at the team hotel – I think it was the Clarion. It was about two blocks from the park and we walked to Busch Stadium and walked back afterwards. St. Louis was doing it up right and there were bands on every corner. There were jazz bands and blues bands and we were hoping the Cardinals would be singing the blues after Game 4. We were trying to become the first expansion team to win a World Series. We made it to the World Series in 1980, but we lost to the Phillies. The Cardinals were going for a record 10th world championship; we're going for our first. This could get interesting.

"Well, it wasn't interesting for long. They had Tudor on the mound and he shut us out 3-0. We got another good pitching performance, but theirs was better. But after the game, the locker room was upbeat. I remember Hal was sitting in front of his locker, and his cap was sitting crazy on his head – like he always wore it – and he said, 'We got those SOBs right where we want them.' He was referring to being down three games to one, just like we were against the Blue Jays. We had one more game in St. Louis and then it was back home to Kansas City, so we had to find a way to win Game 5.

"Willie (Wilson) and I were leaving the locker room, and ABC was hanging the lights and stuff for the next game. They were preparing for all the postgame interviews from the locker room. I'd been in one World Series loser's locker room and I didn't want to be in another one. I asked Willie what we were going to do. He turns to the guy hanging the lights and says, 'You might as well take down those damn lights right now. There won't be any crying in this locker room tomorrow night.' That was so awesome! I was so proud of Willie. I knew we were going to win the fifth game, and we did, 6-1. It was funny, both wins in St. Louis were by the same score, 6-1. Danny Jackson was amazing in Game 5. Charlie (Leibrandt) and Buddy (Black) had each pitched well enough to win, but Sabes and D.J. just rose to the occasion and made sure the series returned back to Kansas City.

"The plane ride home after Game 5 was business as usual. I wish we could have taken a riverboat home or taken a train and stopped at all the little towns along the way. I heard about the dorm room at MU where one side was all Cardinals and the other side was all Royals. The entire state was so excited about this series and so was I. We were down three games to two and knew we were going to win the next two games – we just knew it. Charlie was pitching Game 6 and we had a lot of confidence in him. I was thinking about being a little kid, hitting rocks with a broomstick, dreaming about the World Series, and I was flying home for Game 6. Does life get any more exciting than this? I soon found out it does.

"Pinch-hitter Dane Iorg got the big, two-out hit in the bottom of the ninth inning of Game 6 and we won 2-1 after trailing 1-0 the entire game, and then we come back and win Game 7 11-0. Does life get any better than this? No. It doesn't get any better than winning a World Series, it really doesn't. Now, the rest of the guys on this year's team get to experience that feeling."

CHAPTER 4

A Golden Opportunity

Wally Pipp is the wrong kind of famous.

Pipp had a 14-year career as a Major League Baseball player spanning from 1913-1928. He spent 10 of those seasons with the New York Yankees, inarguably the most famous franchise in the sport. He hit a respectable .281 for his career and twice led the American League in home runs (1916 and 1917).

And, yet, he's most famous for the one game he didn't play.

The legend of Wally Pipp is such the exact circumstances around the Yankees' game versus the Washington Senators on June 2, 1925 are still unknown. The most popular theory is it was a headache. Some believe he was beaned by a pitch during pre-game warm-ups. One of his children believes he was willingly stepping aside for a man he knew would eventually become a giant in the history of the sport.

Whatever the reason, Yankees manager Miller Huggins made the decision to bench Pipp, in favor of an unseasoned youth by the name of Lou Gehrig. From that game forward, "The Iron Horse" would go on to redefine the concept of reliability in sports. Gehrig played in 2,130 straight games, a record that stood until it was broken by Cal Ripken Jr. in 1995.

Now, losing one's position due to off-the-field circumstance and never regaining it is known as being "Pipped." It goes without saying, despite his long career, Wally Pipp is not someone with whom athletes want to be associated.

And so, okay, maybe the story of how Mike Sweeney got his shot with the Kansas City Royals isn't exactly a Wally Pipp – Lou Gehrig story. But it's in the ballpark, at least, and features a sudden retirement, a flying four-wheeler, and a memorable three-run blast.

It's also a secret Sweeney kept until the day of his induction into the Royals Hall of Fame on Aug. 15, 2015.

"Jeff King (a former Kansas City first baseman), was one of my best friends," Sweeney recalled during his induction ceremony. "I still go fly fishing with him in Montana and Jackson Hole. And he told me he was going to retire!"

Sweeney was shocked, and did his best to persuade King to stay. At the time – the first month of the 1999 season – he was a third-string catcher and backup designated hitter. However, he notched a couple of starts under his belt and had done pretty well. He didn't want to see his friend go.

King wasn't having it. His love for the game had long since faded, and in his mind it was time to devote himself to his wife and their seven children. So the day after his pension from Major League Baseball fully vested, May 23, 1999, King said sayonara.

It led to an emotional goodbye for Sweeney, who had no idea his friend's retirement would open the door on his own big break. The day after, as fate would have it, was an off-day for the Royals, and Sweeney and his two roommates, Jed Hanson and Jeremy Giambi, were looking for something to do.

"We thought, well, let's go out before we have to take the bus to the airport and do some fishing at Kevin Appier's farm," Sweeney said. "So we went out there and saw the llamas, the Clydesdales, all the exotic animals that 'Ape' has. I actually fished and caught some bass.

"We said, 'Hey, we better get going. Time to head up to the airport.'"

That was when Giambi noticed a tricked-out four-wheeler, complete with a cage on top.

"He says, 'I used to race these as a kid. I'm going to out and tear this thing up,'" Sweeney continued. "So he goes and rips around Appier's property and goes over an area where there's a cornfield. And he jumps and he lands, barely, on the front wheels. I was like, 'Man, he almost killed himself.'"

They were immediately greeted by the frantic form of Appier's wife, Lorie, who wanted to know when one of their four wheelers had grown a jet engine and wings. Giambi gleefully confessed to being the one to jump the small vehicle, and revved up to do it again. Without a helmet.

"This time, he hits on the top of the cage," Sweeney said. "And I'll never forget it. Jeremy, after flipping three times and hitting the top of the cage again, flipping again and landing on his wheels. We run up to him and there is blood all over his face, all over his body. I'm thinking, 'Oh dear God.' The next thing we know we are in the Paola (Kan.) hospital and Jeremy's getting staples in his skull, stitches in his eye, getting his knees cleaned up."

Naturally, they had to show up for the team flight. Which they did. And, just as naturally, manager Tony Muser was going to take a look at his battered player and want to find out exactly what happened to the man he expected to start first base the next day.

"(Giambi) goes, 'Well, I was changing my oil at Sweeney's house and the toolbox fell off and hit me in the head,'" Sweeney remembered, laughing. "And I told Jeremy, I said, 'I ain't lying for ya.' And until last night I've never shared that story, but I think Jeremy, since he's retired now, would appreciate a good laugh."

The next game was versus the Pittsburgh Pirates on the following Monday. Naturally, with King a sudden retiree and Giambi looking like he belonged in a MASH unit, it was the third-string catcher and backup DH who got the call.

"I went out there and hit a three-run homer," Sweeney said. "Next night hit a couple doubles off the fence. And the rest is history. I took over that job. But had Jeff King not retired and Jeremy Giambi not raced motorcycles as a kid, maybe Royals fans would have never heard of me and we wouldn't be celebrating this great day."

It was a day he was able to share with his wife, Shara, his mother, Maureen, and his father, Mike Sr., who almost died in early May 2015 after complications from esophageal cancer. Mike Sr., a former Angels minor league prospect, walked away from the game he loved to support his family, which he cherished even more. That left a lasting impact on his son, who ranks among the finest players to ever wear Royal blue.

Sweeney counts his Catholic faith as the greatest blessing in his life, followed closely by his wife and their five children. Then comes his father, his mother, and his seven siblings.

"Right after that comes the blessing of being a Kansas City Royal," he said. "When I was 17-years-old, when I signed to be a Royal. I'll never forget that call I got from (longtime director of scouting and fellow Royals Hall of Famer) Art Stewart, who said, 'Son, you've been drafted in the 10th round by the Kansas City Royals.'

"I never dreamt that this day would happen. I thought, 'Man, I'm going to give it everything I can. Maybe play a couple years of minor league ball, just to say I could be like my dad.'

The elder Mike Sweeney played for a couple of seasons, then hung up his cleats permanently to be with his wife and live out a different dream – that of being a family man. And to his namesake, he could have provided no finer example, for Mike Jr. wanted to be just like him. No delusions of grandeur. Just a shot at the big-time and the chance to say he tried, while finding another way to support his family with an honest living.

Photo Courtesy Denny Medley-USA TODAY Sports

Aug 15, 2015; Kansas City, MO, USA; Former Kansas City Royals player Mike Sweeney speaks during his induction ceremony into the Royals Hall of Fame before the game against the Los Angeles Angels at Kauffman Stadium. Sweeney was a rock for the Royals during some of the club's darkest days, providing leadership in the clubhouse as well as all-star caliber play on the field.

What he didn't count on is this whole "pro baseball" thinking sticking around. Even as he progressed through the minor league system he never allowed himself to believe.

"It wasn't until my first big league camp in 1995, when I went to major league camp in Baseball City (Fla.), and that's when the lights clicked for me," Sweeney said. "I'm dressing with guys like Wally Joyner. And I'm doing catching drills with guys like Lance Parrish, Pat Borders, Brent Mayne, Mike Macfarlane – and I'm thinking, man, I have these guys' baseball cards! And I get to share a locker room with them?"

It's fair to say Sweeney was a bit star struck. To him, they didn't wear simple uniforms, they were one step away from being outright super heroes.

But then a funny thing happened. They took batting practice that first spring day, and Sweeney was hitting them just as far – farther in fact – than these guys he so idolized. And sure, maybe he launched a few throws from his position at catcher into center field, but he was throwing it just as quickly as the other guys.

At that point, realization slowly started to dawn within him. He could play. He could excel. His idols weren't so different from him!

"I had 'em way up here," Sweeney noted. "And I thought, man, they wear a cape and a tight suit. They're Royalty. And I'm just, I'm just a backup catcher. But obviously God had other plans for me. He brought some great friends along my side that really encouraged me and pushed me to not only be a better man, but to be a better ballplayer – and I was able to play the game here for 13 years.

"There are very, very few that get selected to be a Hall of Famer. And it's still hard for me to believe I'm it. But today is really going to be one of the greatest days of my life."

It wasn't what he envisioned for himself, because the young Mike Sweeney Jr., as it turns out, didn't give himself enough credit. He was still a family man and gave everything he had to take care of them. He followed his father's example. He just found a different way to do it.

Which is one of the primary reasons why that muggy afternoon in mid-August was so special. His family was there to share it with him. And despite his illness, his father was there to see the culmination of his son's professional career – how tremendously all his hard work had paid off.

The truth is, it was something of a minor miracle Mike Sweeney Sr. was in his reserved seat that day. Diagnosed with esophageal cancer on New Year's Eve 2014, five months later he was in surgery. At first, it seemed as if everything had gone to plan. The surgeon even came out and informed them it had been a complete success.

Five minutes later? Well, that was a different story.

"That same surgeon called us back to the consultation room and told us that everything went wrong," Sweeney said. "He had a heart attack, a collapsed lung, a punctured lung, his kidneys were failing, he had pneumonia, his blood pressure was almost down to nothing."

His father would obviously need additional surgery, and as the surgeon turned to leave the consultation room to prepare, she turned to Mike and advised him that if he happened to be a man of faith, he should find solace in it. Because the family needed to be ready for the worst.

So Mike did. And he sat by his father's side right before they took him away for surgery, and his dad made him a promise to be in his seat, at Kauffman Stadium on August 15th.

"And he kept his promise," Sweeney said. "So even though I am a Royals Hall of Famer officially in a couple hours, I would be nothing without my dad. And I don't even know if I could stand up and receive this great honor had my dad not been here today.

"But he kept his promise."

• • •

Despite his realization that he could play with Big Leaguers, it didn't take long for Sweeney to learn that didn't mean he would.

Hard work in the minor leagues got him a shot at The Show, and for the first few years he kind of "limped around," to hear Sweeney tell it. Those early Royals teams of which he was a part actually had a somewhat staggering amount of talent; talent which unfortunately went elsewhere to continue and conclude their careers. He knew Jermaine Dye could hit the ball farther. He knew Carlos Beltran could run faster. He knew Johnny Damon was the team's best all-around player, and Mike Macfarlane its leader.

So he decided to control what he could control – his work ethic. He vowed nobody would outwork him, and in fact no one did. It was that hard work that led to his breakout season in 1999, during which he hit .322 with 22 home runs and 102 RBI, establishing himself as one of the finest hitters in the American League.

And to think, it almost didn't happen.

As they are wont to do, trade rumors were swirling in the off-season, and many of them seemed to focus on Sweeney. Teams thought he had potential and that meant he had value. This was unwelcome news, as he had just purchased a house in Overland Park, Kan. – not far from Kauffman Stadium – and was 1,500 miles away from his family. He was still a single man at that point. His entire support structure consisted of the friends he had made on the team.

In the midst of the storm, he sought out advice from the most honest source he knew – former Royals pitcher Tom Burgmeier, who at the time was a coach in the organization's minor league system.

"What's about to happen to me, Burgy?" Sweeney asked, nervously.

"Well, you want the truth?" Burgmeier replied.

Sweeney confirmed he did, in fact, want the unvarnished truth.

"Well, I was just in a meeting earlier today at the 'K,' and Mike, they love you as a player but they said you'll never catch another day as a Royal. That your days are numbered as a Kansas City Royal."

Sweeney processed this for a moment, before continuing. "What's the chance of me being a Kansas City Royal this year?"

"Zero percent."

With spring training just a week away, Burgmeier advised him to travel lightly to Baseball City. That was as honest as he could be. Sweeney thanked him and followed his advice, doing his laundry religiously every few days, folding it, and living out of his suitcase. He refused to unpack.

The night after he spoke with Burgmeier, however, he had what he described as "one of the coolest nights of my life."

Sweeney makes no attempt to hide his Catholic Christian faith. He's proud of it. In many ways it defines him. So he visited The Church of the Nativity in Overland Park, and just prayed. He prayed for guidance. He prayed for direction. And as he looked down at his Bible, he noticed a sticker he must have placed without knowing it – one of a tandem bicycle.

To Sweeney, the message was clear. He needed to trust everything to God's hands. His career, his loneliness, his desire to meet his future wife and have a family. All of his plans and dreams needed to be placed in God's hands.

As Sweeney wept softly in the pew, he realized how badly he didn't want to feel anxious or depressed. He didn't want to feel hopeless. All he wanted to do was pedal.

"And when I say pedal, I mean pedal harder than I've ever pedaled in my life," Sweeney said. "And I'm going to trust You with my life, and my career, and my future wife. And although I was ridiculed for a couple years for not dating, my life turned around that night at that church. Because every single day in spring training and every day for the rest of my career, I'd make the sign of the cross and say 'Lord, just let me go out and pedal today.'"

Lo and behold, things got easier. A weight lifted from Sweeney's shoulders. He could be facing Randy Johnson, Pedro Martinez, or Roger Clemens, and he told himself if he just remembered to pedal for the next three hours, he'd be okay. He'd done the work and the preparation. It was just time to move forward.

"It's not that bad," Sweeney said. "Say I'm facing this future Hall of Famer. Well, he's gotta face me. And all I'm going to do is pedal my heart out tonight.

"And I'm so glad that zero percent chance of being a Royal turned into a 100-percent chance," he added. "Tony Muser, (former general manager) Allard Baird, they gave me a chance. And I couldn't imagine my life any different or any better had they not given me that chance that off season, or that spring training."

• • •

In 1999, despite Sweeney's personal success, the Royals as a team achieved a franchise-low winning percentage of .398 - with a record of 64-97. They had become baseball's gold standard for futility since the death of beloved owner Ewing Kauffman in 1993.

During one August game that season, with the Royals 20 games out of first place, Sweeney went tearing around third base (representing the go-ahead run) and crashed into Chicago White Sox catcher A.J. Pierzynski in a vicious collision. He doesn't remember if he was safe or out. He doesn't remember the outcome of the game.

But he remembers those bruises. And he remembers teammate Mark Teahen, acquired in a trade, asking him something that stuck with him.

"Sweeney, how do you do it?" the third baseman asked. "How do you do it?"

The veteran was perplexed. "What do you mean, 'How do I do it?'"

"Man, I've been here for a few weeks and we're 20 games out of the lead. It's 100 degrees out there with 100-percent humidity. You're 30-plus-years-old and you're playing the game like that. How do you do it? I mean, come on!"

The question immediately evoked memories of his youth, wearing not the blue of the Kansas City Royals but an Ontario Mountain View Little League jersey, with his father in the coaches' box. Sweeney hit a ground ball to second base and loafed it, allowing for an easy out. And rarely, if ever, had he seen his dad so angry. Mike Sweeney Sr. didn't allow lollygaggers to play baseball for him. If you played the game, you played the game the right way.

Sweeney looked up at Teahen.

"Mark, the way you play the game should never be dictated by what place you're in, what your batting average is, or how hot it is outside or how many fans are in those stands," he said. "You should play that game as hard as you can every single day because you don't know when that jersey's going to be taken off your back. That's how I play the game."

Through those down seasons, and boy were there some down seasons during the 29-year stretch between playoff appearances in Kansas City, Sweeney kept looking at the Royals championship flags that fly in left field with longing in his eyes. He prayed for the opportunity to contribute to another magical season at Kauffman Stadium. He was a Royal, through and through.

It never materialized for him, but he's taken great pleasure in watching the current team finally raise a new flag, and bring respectability back to Kansas City's brand of baseball.

At times, his own Royals teams were "stacked" offensively. Johnny Damon, Jermaine Dye, Joe Randa, Carlos Beltran, Raul Ibañez – scoring runs was not their issue. Today, Sweeney looks around and sees echoes of that ability on this squad, and then some.

"I'm looking on that field and I'm seeing Hosmer, and I'm seeing Infante, and I'm seeing Moose, and I'm seeing Esky. And I'm looking out in the outfield going 'Man, we got Ben Zobrist and we got Alex Gordon. And we got Lorenzo Cain in center. And, of course, El Capitan, Salvador Perez behind the plate."

It's not difficult for Sweeney to excitedly imagine a future in which this young core stays in Kansas City and makes it the home of dynasties once more.

"If these guys would go to their agents, I don't care whether it's Scott Boras or whoever it is, and say 'Hey, I want to be a Royal!' you could have a dynasty here in Kansas City for a long time. And that was my heartbeat. I wanted to have a team where the fans could say 'This is our team!'"

He paused for a moment, before smiling.

"And they have a team like that today."

CHAPTER 5

The Unsung Hero

There isn't any one hero that stands out from the 1985 World Series Champion Kansas City Royals. Sure, there are those who come to mind immediately, such as World Series MVP Bret Saberhagen, cleanup hitter Frank White, Hall of Fame third baseman George Brett, and Dane Iorg - whose pinch-hit single in the bottom of the ninth inning of Game 6 gave Kansas City a 2-1 victory and made a Game 7 and the world championship possible.

But there are the unsung heroes as well, and chief among them would have to be Danny Jackson. The lefty with the nasty stuff won Game 5 in both the American League Championship Series versus Toronto and then the World Series versus the St. Louis Cardinals. His performances twice helped a team on the brink of elimination stay alive for another day, another game, and another chance at that glittering trophy.

"Jack was mean and nasty," former teammate Willie Wilson said, laughing. "The days he pitched, you didn't want to be around him. And the days he lost you really didn't want to be around him. He did some damage to that clubhouse."

But the former No. 1 draft pick did much more damage on the mound, where he beat Jimmy Key and the Jays 2-0 by scattering eight hits over eight shutout innings in Game 5 of the ALCS.

Late manager Dick Howser rewarded Jackson with the start in Game 1 of the World Series where he was outdueled by Cardinals ace John Tudor in a 3-1 St. Louis victory.

With his team down in the series 3-1, Jackson got the ball in another must-win Game 5 and cruised to a 6-1 victory, setting the stage for two memorable home wins and a world championship.

"Jack deserves a lot of credit, because he won the game we needed to win - Game 5," White said. "We don't win (Games) 6 and 7 unless we win Game 5 in St. Louis."

Jackson said he had some extra motivation to succeed against the Blue Jays.

"I pitched Game 5 with a chip on my shoulder in Toronto because Dick didn't pick me as one of the three starters," Jackson said, as Saberhagen, Buddy Black and Mark Gubicza were selected for the first three games.

"When I got the ball, I wanted to make the most of the opportunity. I don't know if I ever wanted to win a game as badly as that one."

Now, fast forward to Game 5 of the World Series, in which the Cardinals were home and Jackson faced another must-win situation.

"We knew Jack was going to win that game," Wilson said. "And the Series was going back to Kansas City. We gave him a little more offense and he did the rest."

Jackson credits the defense and great leadership for allowing him to make his mark on Royals history.

"I had so much faith in the guys behind me," Jackson said. "After we were down three-games-to-one against Toronto and came back, I knew we could do it again. Those were two of the biggest wins of my career."

He went on to win 23 games for the 1990 World Champion Cincinnati Reds, and appeared in three total World Series. He was on the staff of the 1993 National League champion Philadelphia Phillies.

CHAPTER 6

Riding off into the World Series with 'The Duke'

John Wathan bleeds Royals blue, and has for more than 44 years.

He was a first-round pick in 1971 who played for the Royals from 1976 to 1985. He was a part of every championship team during that period, appearing in 860 games, with a career batting average of .261 to go with 21 home runs and 261 RBI. He had his best season in 1980, the year the Royals first appeared in a World Series, during which he played in 126 games and maintained a .305 batting average. In 1982, he became the first member of the Royals to break a Major League Baseball record when he stole 36 bases, breaking the single-season mark for catchers set by Ray Schalk in 1916 - despite suffering a fractured ankle earlier in the season.

Nicknamed "The Duke," because of his love of John Wayne and his ability to impersonate the Hollywood legend, Wathan went on to coach and manage at the big league level, work as a color analyst on Royals telecasts in 1996 and 1997, and work as a scout and minor league instructor for a number of years. He saw many of today's Royals stars when they were making their way through the team's minor league ranks. He and his wife, Nancy, had two sons - Derek and Dusty – who also played professional baseball. Derek played minor league baseball from 1998 to 2008, while Dusty played briefly for the Royals in 2002 and is currently the manager of the Reading Phillies, an affiliate of the Philadelphia Phillies. Their daughter Dina (Blevins) works in the Royals front office, which makes the 2015 season even more special for Wathan – who talked about the past and present at a noisy rally at Kauffman Stadium before the start of the playoffs.

"Everybody that was a part of that (1985 world championship) team and for all the fans of Kansas City, with that long of a draught, to get back into the World Series 29 years – now 30 years - since we won the division, it's a special feeling," Wathan said. "We went through a lot of down years. And a lot of people, a lot of kids didn't know that the Royals were ever very good at all. The greatest thing to me is having a new generation, maybe even two generations in that long of a period, realize that this is a good baseball city and you see it by everybody that's out here today for the rally and batting practice.

"Dina's been here 10 or 12 years. She's a big part of this organization, working in media relations. I talked about the kids that never knew that the Royals were any good. All of my grandkids now are having fun with it as well. I've got, I'm soon to have eight grandkids because Dina's going to have her second here in January 2016. They're all big Royals fans, as well as Phillies fans because Dusty still works there."

Now, Wathan can enjoy the success of the 2014 and 2015 Kansas City Royals as the same type he experienced as a player, from 1976 to 1985.

"Everybody was talking about how easy it was to get out of the parking lot after a game," he quipped, when talking about the down years. "Not so anymore. It takes a while to get out. But what amazes me is how many of these fans stay for the entire game. Even with a big lead or if you're losing by a lot, they still stay and cheer the Royals on 'til the very end. They're all here for the postgame celebration. The interview on TV. The bucket toss for the guy that's getting interviewed. It's crazy."

Wathan is a part of the legacy that so many of today's players talk about on a regular basis.

"We're not who we are today," third baseman Mike Moustakas said. "Without the guys like George (Brett), Frank (White), Duke and all the great players from the 70s and 80s. We're just so proud that we can make them proud of what we're doing today."

"I was so lucky to be here during those great years," Wathan added. "Timing is everything in baseball and life. And because we didn't make a whole lot of changes every year, I think that helped me stay 10 years. We had such success winning and being in the post season seven out of 10 years, I think that's one of the reasons I was able to stay, along with being able to play a little outfield, and first base and catcher - which you don't see very often anymore. Usually teams have two catchers. We had three a lot of those years because I could play other positions. It was a special time and I feel very blessed. People ask me all the time, 'Do you wish you played today to make the money these guys are making?' And I said, 'Not really,' because the fun we had being in the post season seven out of 10 years, money can't buy that."

While the team got back to, and won, the 2015 World Series, Wathan believes the 2014 Wild Card game played a huge role in the Royals' approach to postseason action.

"That Wild Card game helped this team turn the corner, helped this team believe in itself," he said. "Ned Yost has said it many, many times. That was the defining moment for our post season. If we could come back from 7-3, we can come back from anything. The guys never gave up. They knew they had a chance to win when Salvador got that double down the left field line. It was just an amazing night for the city of Kansas City. It took away those 29 years in a heartbeat. Because of my work in the minors, I know a lot of these guys. I saw them when they first signed and what they were like then and seeing what they are like now. It has been a tremendous transformation for all of them, some more than others. They've grown in size. They've grown in stature. Their ability to slow the game down at the big league level. That's what we talk about a lot in the minor leagues. The game is really fast when you get into pro ball. Even faster when you get to the big league level. These guys have been able to do that. It's been really, really fun. And Dayton Moore is so good about always thanking player development and scouting. Without the amateur scouts who sign these guys, without the pro scouts who look at players for trades and without player development that nurtures and guides these guys through the minor leagues to get them here, we wouldn't be where we are."

The 2015 Royals keep talking about how much they have enjoyed growing up together. While many of the Royals during the previous era were homegrown, others like Hal McRae and Amos Otis came to the Royals in trades, and were important parts of the team for more than a decade.

"You know what, this team really reminds me of the 70s and 80s teams," Wathan said. "Because most of our guys were home grown for the most part. A few key trades - Hal McRae and Amos Otis to name a couple. But a lot of the guys, we were in the minor leagues together. Frank White, George Brett and myself. Jamie Quirk, U.L. Washington. Some of them came through the baseball academy that Mr. Kauffman came up with. A lot of things clicked back then with our talent. And playing together, knowing each other, and pulling together as a unit in the minor leagues helped us to the Big Leagues. Just like all these guys that came up and won at AA and won at AAA Omaha. They're doing the same thing. They learned what it was like to win and be in a championship club which helps them here.

"I think when you've been in the game long enough you realize how hard it is to win at this level given so much talent (in the league). So we celebrate every single win. When I'm sitting with Dayton Moore in his suite up there, we do the same thing after games. We celebrate every single night. Every win is important to get to this point in the season. It's huge to win and the celebration, the togetherness is so special. It never changes. It never gets old. October has always been a special month. So when this happens obviously after all these years it's really, really special. The air is cooler and crisper nights. Crisper days. It just feels like baseball in October – and now November - is the best time in the world."

CHAPTER 7

Those Who Came Before

If the current Kansas City Royals were students, they would be profound masters of history.

While they enjoy sharing all the special regular-season moments and postseason victories with their fans, they are quick to point out the pioneers who carved the path to today's newfound success – players like Royals Hall of Fame pitchers Steve Busby and Dennis Leonard, second baseman Cookie Rojas and of course, Major League Baseball Hall of Fame third baseman George Brett.

"Those are the guys who got it done early on, laid the foundation that we're trying to build on," said first baseman Eric Hosmer, a veritable RBI machine during the 2015 postseason. "We're not where we are today without the great players of the past."

Mike Moustakas, the team's all-star third baseman, agreed.

"It's always great when the guys who played before us come into the locker room or down to spring training," Moustakas said. "George has a million stories and you hear about those teams and all the fun and success they had.

"They have a real legacy, and that's what we want to leave."

Busby has the opportunity to watch baseball on a daily basis as he is on the Texas Rangers broadcast crew.

"The game hasn't changed, the rules haven't changed, but the players have changed," said Busby, who pitched in Kansas City from 1972-80 and who is the only pitcher in Major League Baseball history to throw no-hitters his first two seasons in the big leagues.

"I was 6-foot-2 when I pitched and I was considered a big guy. Today, I'd be a pipsqueak. The players are bigger and stronger and faster and I love what's happening in Kansas City.

"The Royals really shocked a lot of people by making the World Series in 2014, and this year, they proved it wasn't a fluke. They are a great organization and (general manager) Dayton Moore has done a great job building a team that has great defense, a lot of speed, and the best bullpen in baseball.

"And those guys can hit, too. They especially seem to come up with the big hits when they need them."

Rojas is now retired, after serving as a coach, manager and broadcaster following an all-star career in Kansas City.

"You always follow your old team and it's so much fun to see what is happening in Kansas City," said Rojas, who played in Kansas City from 1970-77. "The Royals are doing it the right way and they are doing something we could not accomplish and that's make it to the World Series.

Kansas City Royals Hall of Famer Steve Busby, who is now a broadcaster for the Texas Rangers, was the first pitcher in big league history to throw no-hitters in each of his first two seasons in the pros.

"They play hard and they play the game the way it should be played – with a lot of passion and heart. I know last year everyone in America seemed to fall in love with the team because you could tell how much they enjoyed the game and how much they enjoyed being with each other."

Leonard, who was the pitching coach at Raytown (Mo.) High School for many years, was able to experience the thrill of World Series play, starring for the 1980 Royals who lost a six-game series to the Philadelphia Phillies.

"Making it to the World Series was great," said Leonard, who pitched in Kansas City from 1974-86. "But it doesn't mean as much when you lose. I thought we had a great team, but the Phillies beat us in six games and I still think about that from time to time.

"Now, that I live in the (Kansas City) metro area, I get the chance to see a lot of Royals games. And you have to like this team. I've never seen a team that shares all its success with the fans.

"These guys are out spraying champagne and taking photos with the fans after big wins and that's great."

However, there is one setback to all the team's recent success.

"I used to be able to leave my home in Blue Springs at 6:30, get to the stadium, park and be in my seats at 7," chuckled Leonard, who was the winning pitcher in Game 4 of the 1980 World Series. "But not anymore. It's a parking nightmare out there – but that's what comes from success.

"I guess it was like that back when I played, but I never had to mess with it because I got there so early and left late after the game. It's just great to have Kansas City pride back at Kauffman Stadium."

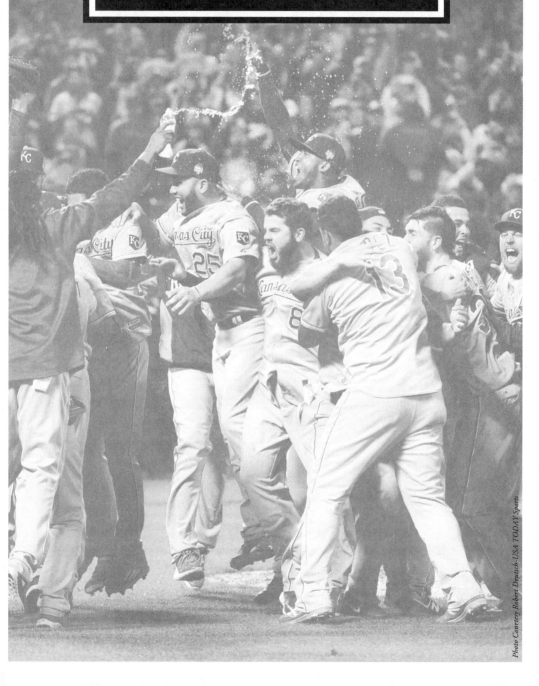

The Guys

CHAPTER 1

The Man with the Golden Glove

The truth is, not a day goes by that Alex Gordon doesn't think about Game 7 of the 2014 World Series.

It's not difficult to understand why. After smoking a two-out triple in the bottom of the ninth inning, finally putting solid wood on a pitch from the seemingly inexhaustible, unhittable Madison Bumgarner, he was just 90-feet from home. Ninety feet from tying the game, and a shot at another of the impossible comeback victories for which the Royals had become known during postseason play.

And 90-feet away he remained, as Bumgarner coolly forced Royals catcher Salvador Perez – the hero of the 2014 Wild Card game – into a pop-up in foul territory, giving the San Francisco Giants not just the third out, but their third World Series title in five years.

"A tough way for it to end," Gordon recalled, in typical understated fashion. "But it was pretty special to make the postseason. Me being here for a long time, with all the struggles, all the frustration that we went through. It was all worth it, you know? It was some kind of special, and I think it's motivated us (in 2015) to get back there and get that same feeling again."

The eight consecutive playoff wins and punched-ticket to just the third World Series appearance in the history of the franchise meant as much to Gordon as any of his younger teammates. He struggled through ups and downs from 2007 to 2014 that saw him demoted to the minors, asked to change positions, and caused him to wonder if he was ever going to live up to the lofty expectations pressed upon him by his status as the team's top draft pick – and the second pick overall – in the 2005 First-Year Player Draft.

"You know, it meant the world and to do it with some of the guys, not only me, but some of the guys that were involved in (my) time over the years," Gordon explained. "The (Luke) Hochevars, the Billy Butlers . . . Dayton Moore was here the whole time. Billy was here, but unfortunately he's not here anymore (signed by the Oakland A's prior to the 2015 season), but you know, he got to experience that before he left. So yeah, it was something special. I know when we clinched (a spot in the 2014 Wild Card game) in Chicago, me, Hoch, and Billy took a picture just because it felt like we were the guys who were here through the struggles, through the down years. And to finally reach the playoffs and the World Series - it was the weight of the world off our shoulders and it was so, so much fun."

Though the more youthful Royals fans of today might not remember, there have been some pretty successful teams to take the field at what is now Kauffman Stadium. But there might not have been any who seemed to enjoy each other's presence more. Pundits talk an awful lot about team chemistry being a key component of winning ballclubs, and whatever it is the Royals have it in spades.

"Yeah, for sure," Gordon agreed. "I mean, we're a tight-knit group here. We all get along. I know we always say we have good chemistry. But we really do. We're all pulling for each other. We all get along off the field. And sometimes that's not always the case. I've been on teams where some guys don't get along with other people. Over the past few years that has changed. Maybe it's the leadership in here, the guys Dayton's brought in here; but everyone gets along really well. Everyone's fighting for the same thing, and that's winning games every day."

Gordon was once the No. 1 college baseball player in the nation, a budding superstar from the University of Nebraska, but the flame that burned on his "potential" guttered out after a couple of lackluster seasons. He knew he needed to make some important decisions if he wanted to stay in the big leagues. It all began with surgery and a move from third base to left field that gave new life to a comatose infield career.

"Ever since my hip surgery is when it kind of started," a thoughtful

Gordon said. "You know I had my hip surgery and then I came back really quick and never had the movement that you see Moose do on a daily basis. I kinda lost the confidence when I wasn't getting the balls. And I was just, just struggling. So 2010 came around and you know, I had that broken finger, so once again a setback. I think Dayton kinda knew that was I frustrated and things weren't working out (at third) and he thought for my sake and the team's sake, it would be best for me to move to the outfield. It was two weeks into 2010 season, so it was kinda something that surprised me. Something that I didn't know was coming. When it happened, obviously, I wouldn't say I was upset, just shocked a little bit. I realized this isn't what I had planned when I got drafted. You know, No. 2 overall for the Royals. But you know what, life gives you challenges. And I wasn't the first guy to ever get sent down, so I kinda looked at it that way and said, 'Hey this is a challenge and I gotta work hard to get back where I need to be. Go down there with a positive attitude and you know. Head up. And do the best that I know how to.'

Photo Courtesy Jeff Curry-USA TODAY Sports

Oct 27, 2015; Kansas City, MO, USA; Kansas City Royals left fielder Alex Gordon hits a solo home run against the New York Mets in the 9th inning in Game 1 of the 2015 World Series at Kauffman Stadium. A hometown hero, Gordon has developed a penchant for clutch hitting during his career. This home run may have been his biggest moment yet.

"And it's all worked out pretty well. I'm always striving not to be satisfied. I think on a daily basis, some guys might come in and take a day off, but I really feel like I come in here every day trying to get better as an outfielder. Shagging out there, talking to Rusty (Kuntz, the Royals first base coach who worked in Omaha with Gordon). Something new always comes up. So it's, I think, never being satisfied by where you're at and just always striving to get better. That's kinda how I view it.

"But it wasn't easy. It wasn't until 2011 that I felt like a big league outfielder. In 2010 I struggled in Triple A. Not a lot of people saw it, but there were a lot of mistakes – a lot – and there were a lot of the Triple A pitchers who didn't like me for a good period of time. But even when I came back I was still making some minor mistakes that you know, typical big league outfielders didn't make. Once I got a full season, 2011, under my belt, a full spring training under my belt, when I got to feeling healthy – that's when I started feeling good. Play after play. Every time I made a play, I felt like my confidence got better and better. That was definitely how I felt throughout the 2011 season."

Gordon is now considered the premier left fielder in all of baseball. He is a fearless Gold Glove winner who has no concern for his personal well-being, as he crashes into outfield walls, dives into the stands and lays it all on the line for his teammates and the fans.

"I always say I'm a football player in a baseball player's body," he said, chuckling. "I'm a football player on a baseball team. I grew up playing football. I was a safety and I loved delivering on the hits. So I guess I carried that over to baseball. I just enjoy making plays and when it's running into a wall, I know it's going to hurt. But I realize that the pain will go away. So I just enjoy making plays and helping my pitchers out any way I can. And honestly, I'm still learning out there. There are tough plays – catching the balls in the sun on day games. It's something I've really had to learn. First season, 2011, I didn't know really how to get the ball out of the sun. Same with the lights at every stadium. Every stadium's different. You gotta find ways to move your body and know before the pitch is thrown where it's at and what you need to do if that situation occurs. So, I kinda learned it from (former teammate) David DeJesus. If you ever watch him with a ball in the sun, how he turned his body and really made those adjustments. You know, I kinda learned it from him and obviously Rusty taught me a little bit.

"I feel like I'm pretty good at it now. But it's still a challenge. People ask me about the warning track and if I notice it – I guess because I'm always jumping into the wall to make a catch. I've played here for so long that even if we didn't have the track I'd probably know where I was at. But yeah, it definitely helps when you're at full speed and you're running to the wall, but I usually don't slow down anyways, so it definitely helps to know where you're at once you feel that dirt. But I'm still going to do all I can do to make a catch and get an out."

Gordon's biggest fan is his 4-year-old son, Max, who ran into a wall emulating one of his father's recent catches that saw him dive into the fence in front of the Royals bullpen.

"There are 29 other outfielders in baseball," pitcher Jeremy Guthrie said. "Who don't make that catch."

"That was just funny," Gordon said, with a smile. "I mean, my wife actually sent me a video so I got it on my phone. He got done taking a bath and obviously he watched the game. And he just runs as hard as he can into the wall and falls down and lays there for about 10 seconds and as he's doing it he says, 'Alex Gordon makes this great catch!' Just something kid's do. It's really hilarious! I guess everyone pays attention to the big catches."

So many years of frustration for fans and players came to an end in 2014 when the Royals reached the postseason for the first time in 29 years. But first, they had to get past the Oakland A's in a Wildcard game that is now part of Major League Baseball lore – and Gordon certainly played his part.

"Well, you know, the one game playoff is a tough way to go and when you have a game like we had you kinda experience all the emotions and all the things you have to deal with in the playoffs," he explained. "So after that game was over, it was like nothing else could phase us really, except for I guess (San Francisco Giants pitcher Madison) Bumgarner. But that game just really gave us a lot of confidence and a feeling like we deserve to be here after that game's over. And I think you saw it when we swept the Angels and then swept Baltimore. Two very good teams. But we played our best baseball at the right time.

"That Wild Card game was crazy. The best part was coming out before the game and just seeing that crowd and that atmosphere. That's something you work for throughout the 162-game season to get to that point. And the satisfaction of having that atmosphere and that energy, but during the games, there's a lot of ups and downs. A lot of emotions going from high to low, but I think that we stuck together. That's what a good team does. And we found a way to win. Even when we were down 7-3 in the seventh, we were fine.

"We knew we were up against a lot of bad odds with (Jon) Lester throwing and being down like that, but knew we weren't going to lose. We knew they were the team that I think everyone was expecting to win and once we got down we were hey, the season's going to be over unless we do something about it. And everyone kinda looked at each other and said, 'Hey, let's do something about it.' And in the 12th, Sal gets the hit and it's just joy. I mean, I was just happy as anyone could be and happy to see Sal get the hit. He'd had a tough game going at bat, and that's just baseball. You just never know when your name's going to be called and you can be the hero. That's what Sal was that day. It just speaks about the game of baseball. You just gotta move on after everything happens 'cause this game is about failure and that's what he did. He stayed positive and kept playing and became the hero."

Gordo's Top 5 Defensive Gems

"This was really kind of fun, going back and picking my Top 5 personal defensive plays."

- My top play came in 2012 at Minnesota, robbing Danny Valencia of a home run. That was definitely No. 1.
- No. 2 was 2015 in Chicago, jumping into the stands. People ask me if I got hurt on that play and the guy wearing the black (Chicago) jersey kind of broke my fall. The fans were pretty good to me after the catch.
- No. 3 was in Seattle throwing, out (Kyle) Seager at home plate. It was extra innings so, it kept the game going. We were in a playoff race so it was pretty special.

- No. 4 was the playoff day game against Baltimore here. Making a catch, running into the wall.
- And then No. 5 was probably here playing Oakland. (Josh) Reddick hit a fly ball. I ran, caught it, fell down and threw somebody out at home plate and he ran over (former Royals catcher) Brayan Pena and it was a double play.

CHAPTER 2

The Wizard of Hoz

The sun pounds the infield at Kauffman Stadium as Jarrod Dyson and Paulo Orlando take their hacks during an optional batting practice, late in a memorable 2015 season in which the Royals would go on to claim the best record in the American League.

They are soon joined by a third teammate, who grabs a bat and begins knocking baseballs off the wall in left, center and right field.

Photo Courtesy Brad Penner–USA TODAY Sports

Nov 1, 2015; New York City, NY, USA; Kansas City Royals first baseman Eric Hosmer reacts after hitting a RBI double against the New York Mets in the 9th inning in Game 5 of the World Series at Citi Field. Hosmer was a late-innings hero during the 2015 playoffs, amassing RBI at a rate surpassed only by New York Yankees legend Lou Gehrig.

Eric Hosmer might be the last player anyone would expect to take optional batting practice, but that's why he's among the best hitters in baseball.

"He works hard," manager Ned Yost said. "That home run he hit last night (an opposite field blast that might be orbiting our planet) was something else. He has so much power to the opposite field. He's made himself a complete hitter."

In the same way George Brett grew from a timid rookie to the voice of the team, Hosmer has accepted the torch from the Hall of Fame third baseman and is now the face of the 2015 World Series champions.

"I don't know if I'd go that far, but I enjoy talking about our games and anytime you're mentioned in the same sentence with George Brett, well, that's pretty special," Hosmer said. "I want to be here for everyone. I enjoy talking about this team. Last year was special and we want this year to be just as special. We're still hungry, still scrapping for wins. We'll be hungry and scrapping for wins until the final out of the season – and we all hope that's after we win Game 7 of the World Series."

Of course, as everyone knows by now, it was. The Royals emerged victorious from a postseason that saw them engineer so many late-inning comeback victories they came to be almost expected.

If Hosmer isn't hitting awe-inspiring homers, he's making the type of plays at first base that rival those gems made by fellow Gold Glove winners Alex Gordon and Lorenzo Cain.

"You see a ball hit and think it's heading to right field," Yost said. "And Hoz snags it. He makes the plays he's supposed to make and the plays he's not supposed to make."

Added all-star shortstop Alcides Escobar: "If you get (the throw) anywhere near Hoz at first base, he's going to catch it. He's the best, man. I think everyone on the infield has more confidence because Hoz catches everything at first."

Hosmer is the man young ladies in Kansas City want to marry; he's the face of the team that every dad dreams of his daughter dating. He has the movie star good looks and personality of a budding superstar who feels comfortable in Kansas City. Every night on the Jumbotron there are the signs: "Future Mrs. Hosmer," "Eric, We Ditched Our Husbands –

Come Party with Us After the Game," and the fan favorite "The Wizard of Hoz."

"Yeah, I see the signs," he said, grinning shyly. "Thank you, ladies. I like the signs. We check them out from the dugout, you bet. Our fans have made the past two seasons so special. The young guys on this team all came up together and we wanted to give something special to the fans who had waited 29 years to get to the postseason. We always knew this was a baseball town, and we consider the fans our 10th man. We don't win a lot of games last year without them. We sure don't win the Wild Card game (a 9-8, 12-inning, heart-attack inducing victory, in which they trailed 7-3 versus Oakland and postseason icon Jon Lester in the seventh inning) without them. Even when we were down four runs, they kept cheering and we fed off that. And when we won, we wanted to share the celebration with them."

Hosmer and his teammates returned to the field and posed for photos and sprayed champagne on the fans after that Wild Card game. They later celebrated with the fans at the Power & Light District when Hosmer tweeted that he and his teammates were going to savor the biggest win of the past three decades.

Now, it's his time to talk about what it's like to be Eric Hosmer, and naturally, he starts by thanking general manager Dayton Moore and the Royals organization for making so many dreams become a reality.

"It's a process that is basically a common factor in Major League Baseball now," Hosmer said. "A

Kansas City Royals first baseman Eric Hosmer reaches up high to make another fan's day. The young native of Miami is a former first-round draft pick of the Kansas City Royals, and part of a group of homegrown talent developed by the organization that is now coming into its own.

lot of teams have the wave of young prospects and players that have come through their system and basically they all get up to the Major Leagues together and with the way the contracts work and all that, it's a window that a lot of these teams have to take advantage of. Here in Kansas City, when we were all getting drafted and going through the minor leagues, the pitch to us was that they're basically starting over.

"They're trying to build through their minor league system and have us be that core group of Major League players who can not only make the playoffs in Kansas City one year, but make Kansas City – the Royals organization – a powerhouse. And make them an organization and a team that's right up there in the standings every year, and a team that Major League Baseball expects to be in postseason play every year."

All the talk, all the hopes and dreams, culminated in a stunning two-year run, that saw the Royals not just make the playoffs and push the World Series to a decisive Game 7 in 2014, but kick down the door in 2015. It was a season in which the Royals possessed the best record in the American League, won the Central Division, and displayed an inexhaustible supply of grit en route to becoming World Series champions.

"When you leave spring training every year with your roster and your group of guys, everyone makes a commitment that you're sold on for the whole entire season," Hosmer said. "Baseball is a game of failure, and before you leave spring training you are going to have 50 wins and 50 losses pretty much no matter what heading into the season. So, you know, a big thing that we had to learn was how to deal with failure, so you know it's one thing to come and lose a game and then everyone's down, but right when you walk out of that clubhouse you really gotta flush it out and move on and just be prepared for the next day.

"I think that we treat wins like that, the same thing. We enjoy 'em while it happens but as soon as we walk out of the clubhouse, we flush it out and, you know, it's right back to preparing for the next game, the next task at hand. So, I think we never panic, and the reason why we are so laid back it seems like to everybody, is because we are believers that this group of guys in here can, over the course of 162 games, be elite. So for us, if we lose two, three games in a row there's no need to stress about it and make it a bigger deal than it is. Because we are confident enough that we can bounce back and you know, win three games in a row; it's just that easy."

In 2014, when a young Royals team realized that they had the talent to make a legitimate run at the playoffs, they began taking losses to heart. Sometimes too strongly. A tough loss would carry over to the next game. That's when fun-loving catcher Salvador Perez finally put on a smile, turned up the music and reminded everyone that they play a game – and playing a game is supposed to be fun.

"After you win, every game everybody comes and puts music on and it's the most fun thing ever to do," Hosmer explained. "You have music blasting and you're in a clubhouse with a bunch of guys you enjoy being around. And we were on a great run, won 10 of 11 games and I just remember coming in to the locker room and no one is talking, and everyone is upset right after the game.

"And Salvy just kinda put music on and said 'There's no reason to be down.' We needed to do what we had been doing and the way we had been doing it. We had been playing some phenomenal baseball, so there's no reason to be down. And really it just characterizes the mood and the character we have on this team.

"You realize you're competing against the best guys in the world and no one's perfect. And you're going to have nights where you

Eric Hosmer has helped lead the charge among his fellow Royals to bring their excitement and enthusiasm to the fanbase – and their efforts have paid off in a big way. The Kansas City community is more invested in the Royals than ever before, as the more than 800,000 fans who showed up to the victory parade in downtown Kansas City can attest.

think you're ready to perform, but it just doesn't happen on the field. So the faster you can move on from it, and be ready to go the next day, we feel the better off you are."

In the mid 1970s through the 1980s, when the Royals won seven division titles and appeared in two World Series, the locker room was their sanctuary. Guys got there early and left late. They would sit by their lockers and talk about the game for hours upon end. In recent years, this young team has emulated those veterans and the end result is much the same – wild success.

"I totally agree," Hosmer said. "We enjoy it each and every day and especially toward the end. Especially going into the postseason and going in that whole run and anywhere you go, just seeing the amount of people supporting you in the city and it just makes you realize that not only is this special to us, but this is special to a lot more people than we all know. And they've been waiting for this for a long time and I just think the group of guys we have in here, and the personalities, and just how many fun guys we have in here; I think it was the perfect match for a fan base who has been patiently waiting so long for their team to bring some joy to Kansas City. To make them enjoy coming to the stadium.

"We want our fans to enjoy coming to the stadium as much as we enjoy it. I think you mix that with a group of young guys who enjoy playing this game like they're 12-years-old and really embrace the atmosphere here, then you get something special. Embrace the people in the stands that love, whether they are 40-years-old or they're 20-years-old, to come to the ballpark and scream as loud as they can for their team. I just think it's a great match."

Royals Hall of Fame second baseman Frank White personifies the type of Kansas City baseball hero who shares his success with his fans. Time permitting, he will sign an autograph for every fan in sight. Yet when talking about the 1985 championship, he said he wished that the team would have shared more of the memorable moments with the fans. White wished for a moment like that following the 2014 Wild Card victory, when several of the players – following Hosmer's lead – invited fans down to Kansas City's raucous Power & Light District to party together and revel in the victory.

"Yeah, that was a good night," Hosmer said. "You know me, (Johnny) Giavotella, and Dyson were all living together, and we were driving home. We had just gotten done popping champagne here and going out on the field and celebrating with everybody. And we were talking about how cool it was to go out into the stadium and celebrate with 40,000 people. We felt like it would be fun to get to celebrate with them, because if you felt the energy and the passion that just oozed throughout this stadium during that time last year it almost felt like they gave us an advantage."

Hosmer and the Royals quickly realized the atmosphere at a charged-up Kauffman Stadium wasn't something that could be replicated simply by filling a stadium with people.

"You know, when we went to L.A. and played the playoff games there, it's a fun atmosphere but it doesn't even compare to what it was here," he noted. "So we're on the line and we're listening to the National Anthem and you listen to their lineups being called out and you hear their fans booing you and it doesn't really phase you. Because you hear what the other teams go through at Kauffman Stadium and you're just like, 'Oh my God. That's uh, that's quite the boo there,' and you truly feel that everyone, every person that bought a ticket is standing up booing at the top of their lungs. We felt like they're a part of what we did, so we just want to enjoy it with them, all together."

CHAPTER 3

Moose!

Just when you thought it was impossible to love Mike Moustakas any more than his adoring fans already do, the Kansas City Royals' All-Star third baseman goes out and buys a puppy.

When Royals vice president of communications and broadcasting Mike Swanson was searching for Moustakas – following an early-season 5-1 victory over the Pittsburgh Pirates in which Moose had clubbed a mammoth home run – pitcher Danny Duffy said, "Moose is out on the field with Gus."

Swanson just grinned and walked out of the locker room onto the field, where Moustakas was romping with his 2-month-old miniature Australian shepherd. Soon, Moustakas entered the locker room carrying Gus. He deposited Gus in Duffy's lap – although Kendrys Morales soon grabbed him for a quick snuggle – and began a heartfelt conversation with the group of reporters around his locker.

Moustakas is one of a handful of Royals who have the green light on a 3-0 pitch, and manager Ned Yost said following the game, "When Moose saw the green light his eyes lit up."

When that comment was relayed to Moustakas, he grinned and nodded in agreement.

"They did light up because I was looking fastball, and that's what I got," Moustakas said. "It was a fastball."

Enough said. Moustakas turned on the pitch and deposited it onto the steps that lead to the patio bar above the visitors bullpen in deepest right field. It was his 10th home run – marking the fourth year in a row he has hit 10 or more home runs. But what made this season so special is the way Moustakas learned to hit the ball to all parts of the field.

Early on, teams would put on the "Moustakas Shift," moving three infielders to the right side of the field. Moustakas laid down a few bunts – which were guaranteed base hits – but even more impressively, he has learned to hit the ball everywhere. He became more than just a pull hitter.

"I don't know if you realize how tough that is," manager Ned Yost said. "I tried to hit to the opposite field. Believe me, I tried. And I couldn't do it. He has worked hard and reinvented himself as a hitter, and he's done it at this level. It's pretty amazing."

Royals third baseman Mike Moustakas takes his mind off the pressures of the game of baseball by working on his putting game in the Royals clubhouse.

What is even more amazing is the simple fact that Moustakas was hitting a buck-fifty and some change last year when fans were voting for the American League All-Star team. This year, he was the winner of the final fan vote with an amazing 19 million votes cast from around the country.

Now, fans bring Moose antlers to Royals games to celebrate their favorite son. "Forever Royal" might be the team slogan, but fans enjoy crying, "The Moose is Loose!" with equal gusto.

When he catches a pop up, fields a ground ball or steps to the plate, "Moooooose!" resonates throughout The K.

When he smashes a three-run bomb, the noise is deafening.

"We have the best fans anywhere," said Moustakas. "I get chills every game. My job is playing baseball, and it's the greatest job in the world.

"If I can do something that gives our fans something to cheer about, something to make them smile and feel a little bit better, that makes my job even more special."

As the mob of reporters around his locker began to thin out, Moustakas asked a clubhouse attendant if he'd like to take Gus for a walk on The Plaza.

"The ladies love Gus," Moustakas said, as everyone cracked a smile.

The ladies may love Gus, but everyone loves the Moose. And leading the charge is his manager, who can't stop talking about how his talented young infielder re-invented himself.

"Last year his strength was pulling the ball," Yost said. "And he didn't have a lot of success as we had to send him down to the minors to work on some things. This year, his first homer is to the opposite field (it was Moustakas' first-ever major league opposite-field homer). This year, they have to pitch him differently. Last year, when he tried to pull everything he kept popping up pitches. This year, he can stay back, bring his hands in and drive the ball the opposite way. When he gets his pitch—boom—he can hit it into the seats. He's becoming a more complete, well-rounded offensive player."

Hitting coach and big-time Moustakas fan Dale Sveum agreed.

"I've never seen a kid do what he's done," said Sveum, a hitting guru who has turned the Royals into one of the most dangerous offensive teams in the league. "It's hard, really hard. And it takes a lot of work on his part. I'll make some suggestions, and we talk about hitting just about every day, but this (newfound success) is all because of his work ethic and his natural talent. He is a complete big-league hitter."

Moustakas began his remarkable transformation in the 2014 playoffs, where he hit a team-record five home runs, including the game winner in Game 1 of the ALDS in Los Angeles.

"Every kid in Little League hits a home run and dreams about hitting it in the World Series," Moustakas said. "I don't have a World Series home run, but I've been lucky in the playoffs. We'll see what happens. But the homers aren't important. All any of us care about is winning."

The winning took place in 2015 as he played a huge role in the Royals' second world championship, when Kansas City claimed a five-game series from the New York Mets. No homers – but he's getting a ring.

And his postseason heroics the past two seasons are a big reason the cry, "Mooooooooooose!" rings throughout home and away stadiums every time he makes a big play. His 11th-inning home run in Angel Stadium gave the Royals a 3-2 victory over the Los Angeles Angels in the 2014 ALDS opener, and he tacked on another in Kansas City's 8-3 series clincher.

Moustakas' two-run home run capped a three-run 10th inning that gave the Royals an 8-6 victory over Baltimore in the 2014 ALCS opener. He hit a tie-breaking homer in the fourth inning of Game 2 and laid down a key sacrifice bunt in a two-run ninth that pushed Kansas City toward a 6-4 victory.

But his crowning moment – a moment that has been captured in the ultimate tribute of a collectible bobblehead – came with his diving catch in Game 3 of the 2014 ALCS . Baltimore's Adam Jones hit a high, twisting pop foul that was drifting toward the third base dugout suite, where Moustakas made a diving catch.

"That's the best, one of the best catches I have ever seen," said shortstop

Photo Courtesy Robert Deutsch-USA TODAY Sports

Oct 31, 2015; New York City, NY, USA; Kansas City Royals third baseman Mike Moustakas throws to first base against the New York Mets in the second inning in Game 4 of the World Series at Citi Field. Moustakas' solid play at the hot corner has made him an invaluable piece of the infield, and his revamped hitting approach solidified him as an all-around star during the 2015 season.

Alcides Escobar, who had a great view of the play. "Just unbelievable."

Yost called it a game changer.

"People don't understand how important it is for a pitcher to get that first out," Yost said. "To have plays like that is huge. That turns around the entire inning."

Moustakas simply wanted to make the out – and thank the fans who cushioned his fall.

"I could have fallen flat on my face, because I had to kind of twist back to catch the ball," an appreciative Moustakas said. "The people in the suite helped me up the entire way, they didn't let me fall, and they kind of lifted me up out of there – kind of like crowd surfing.

"They just lifted me up, right out of the suite. That was pretty cool."

It sure was, but it's not quite as "cool" as his new approach at the plate. He's not a video or a sabermetrics guy – he's a good, ol' fashioned hard worker who would fit comfortably into any lineup of any team in baseball.

"People ask about my success hitting to all fields, and I just changed my approach," Moustakas said. "You know when it gets to certain counts I try to see a pitch and try to drive it to left field. When I get into other counts I'm trying to pull the ball and it just depends on what the pitch is and where it's located and still not trying to do too much. Again, trying to just get a good pitch, use my hands, put a good swing on it."

"We like to say that we do anything to keep the line moving," Moustakas added, a phrase which was practically the team mantra during the 2015 postseason. "We go out there and do anything we can to win a ball game. It doesn't matter where it comes from. Whether it's 1-0 and our starter does a great job and we get it to bullpen. Or if we have to grind it out for 14 innings. We are gonna go out and try to find a way to win. We believe in each other and I think that's the big thing. We have so much faith in each other and that someone's gonna get the job done at some point.

"And our fans have a lot to do with our success. The fans have just continuously come out every game. Take a Tuesday, where you're not supposed to have many fans, and we're sold out. I mean, the stadium is packed. It's electric. We have a great time playing in front of them. And we love playing for the fans. You know, they're always with us. It gives us a little extra energy you need especially later on in the season, when your body's a little tired. They come out. They get loud and we respond to that. We go out there and we play hard for them.

"And we play hard for each other, too. I think you saw it when we were in Boston (Aug. 23, 2015). That ninth inning, that crazy ninth inning. Omar gets thrown out at home and then we rallied. (Backup catcher Drew) Butera put it together, a great at bat. Didn't try to do too much. Esky the same way. Then the line up just went through. I mean, no one tried to do too much. Base hit here, base hit there – keep the line moving. Then we end up scoring four. That's how much confidence we have in each other. We believe that if you don't get the job done, the next guy's going to get the job done."

While the Royals have complete faith in each other, they also have complete faith in their general manager, Dayton Moore.

"Dayton's done a great job especially late in the season getting (Johnny) Cueto and (Ben) Zobrist in here," Moustakas said. "Cueto is a legitimate ace, the best. Zobrist is unbelievable. Every time you look up, the guy is on base or getting a big hit or making a great play at second base. And even during the off season getting Kendrys and Rios – it's been awesome to be a Royal. I remember when (Mike) Sweeney said a couple weeks ago, every day's a great day to be a Royal, and especially right now. What Dayton's been doing, getting guys in here, finding guys that fit perfectly in this clubhouse with their character, I mean, it's been fun and it's gonna be awesome to see how far we ride this thing out."

Two straight World Series appearances. A World Series championship in the trophy case.

How about another?

• • •

But this season was about more than just baseball for Mike Moustakas. More than just about becoming an All-Star, more than a refined hitting approach. More than a World Series title.

Connie Moustakas was a cheerleader, a scorekeeper, a taxi driver, a cook, a fan and most of all – Connie Moustakas was the No. 1 fan or her son, Mike. And on Aug. 29, she succumbed to a long battle with cancer – a loss which devastated the young star.

"I played baseball, football, and basketball growing up and my sisters played soccer, softball, basketball, and volleyball, and it felt like she was at every single game no matter what," he said. "I had three sisters doing that, and myself, and I don't think she missed one sporting event between all of us. She was always there. Always cheering. Always had a slice of orange during half time or in between innings or what not. Yeah, she was that mom that was always there and not just for us. She was always there for everybody. Everybody always felt like my mom was a second mom to them. So they were able to lean on her when they needed to."

Now, when he needs inspiration, he looks skyward.

"You know, playing is kind of an escape for me," Moustakas said. "Every time I step on the field I get away from everything. I'm able to play baseball and it's my escape from real life actually. I go out there and play ball and kinda escape the world for three or four hours, come back in here and then kind of reflect on everything. I know my mom's out there watching me every day, so (I) just try and go out there and make her proud every single day I step on the field.

"But I think about her all the time. Every time I just catch myself looking around, I'm probably thinking of my mom. How proud of me she would be right now and to see her son out there playing Major League Baseball. She was proud of me when I made it to the big leagues. She was proud of me when I got drafted. She was proud of me when I got my first hit in tee-ball. She's always been proud of me and she'll always be proud of me even though she's not here."

The last time Moustakas saw his mother in the hospital, she was wearing some special gear.

"Yeah," he said, grinning while rubbing his hand through his hair, "She was wearing my All-Star jersey. That was awesome. To be able to share that with her and the rest of my family. To take my All-Star Game jersey home to her was a pretty special moment. I remember her walking around wearing my jersey. All of her doctors were saying how much she'd been talking about it and stuff. So it was a pretty cool memory and it was awesome to be able to share that with her."

There isn't a more tough-nosed player in the big leagues than Connie Moustakas' son. It was his fiery tirade leading into the eighth inning of

Game 4 of the 2015 ALDS that helped the Royals overcome a 6-2 deficit and claim a 9-6 victory.

"I guess I have a little bit of my mom's personality. She was a fighter. Hard-nosed. Always. In everything she did. She never quit and never let us quit. She made sure I was at every single game, every single practice – on time. If I was five minutes early, I was still late by her standards. She always got me and my sisters there, too. That's one thing about her – she made sure that all of us got to where we needed to go. She and my dad did a phenomenal job of doing that and you couldn't ask for a better mother."

Connie was too sick to watch her son play in the postseason in 2014, but Moustakas knew she was there in spirit.

"I look up and thank her when I do something out on the field," he said. "My mom was always a gamer. Even when she was sitting there cheering for us, she was a gamer. There's not just one that really stands out. We used to go play travel ball and travel across the country, and being able to just spend time in different places with her, you know Louisiana – all over. Just hang out. That was my favorite memory. Just hanging out after a game and having a hotdog and a Pepsi. She always had a Pepsi in her hand, which was awesome."

Moustakas paused, and lost himself in thought for a moment.

"She was just the best."

CHAPTER 4

Baseball's Happiest Warrior

Kansas City center fielder Lorenzo Cain was in the middle of World Series Media Day 2014 – an interesting little session where players are seated at tables, complete with oversized placards that state their names – talking about the role defense played in his magical postseason run.

"I know if I think I'm going to get a hit, and someone makes a great play and robs me of a hit, it kills the energy. That's why defense has been so important for us this season," Cain said, as a mysterious water bottle suddenly emerged among the sea of microphones. He didn't need to look up because he knew that his buddy, Royals All-Star catcher Salvador Perez, was on the other end.

"Are you nervous my friend, around all these cameras?" asked Perez, as Cain and the media corps broke out in laughter.

Royals All-Star catcher Salvador Perez has become a favorite among fans, media, and his teammates, thanks to his jovial nature and seemingly inexhaustible supply of energy. Perez took home the 2015 World Series Most Valuable Player Award, and was also awarded yet another Gold Glove at the end of the season, signifying his status as the best defensive catcher in the American League.

Cain looked up and said, "He's a big baby – no, not a baby – oh, get out of here. I'll talk to you in the clubhouse."

To which Perez replied, with the timing of a standup comic, "Give me a hug."

Cain, who could not stop laughing, shooed Perez away, "No hugs! We'll talk in the clubhouse."

Who would have thought that the most imposing figure on the Royals, their 6-foot-3, 245-pound catcher, would also be the most fun-loving member of the team?

"We love Sal," said another Royals player who is soaking in the postseason spotlight like a sponge, Mike Moustakas. "No one is having more fun in the playoffs than Sal – and believe me, we're all having fun."

Added first baseman Eric Hosmer: "Every day I look up Sal's tweets. They kill me, they are so funny. He's just a great teammate and a great guy to be around."

Even stoic manager Ned Yost manages a grin when talking about the best young catcher in baseball.

"Sal is the most fun-loving guy you could ever be around," Yost said. "The guys on the team love him, we all love him."

And Perez isn't just entertaining players and fans with his wit and charm; he's made an impact on the field, too.

He drove in the winning run in that 12-inning, 9-8 Wild Card game masterpiece over the Oakland A's, hit the Royals' first 2014 World Series homer and clubbed a two-run double during the key five-run sixth inning in a 7-2 Game 2 victory.

"I am loving this," Perez said. "This is the World Series. This is my dream. I am having so much fun."

At the time, all anyone could think was, "If he's having this much fun without a World Series title, what will it be like when he finally gets his ring?"

That question was answered in 2015, when he was named the World Series MVP. He looked like an over-sized Little Leaguer when he was handed the MVP trophy in the visitor's clubhouse at Citi Field. If he could have placed a chain around the trophy and worn it on his neck, he would have. He went from baseball's happiest warrior to a World Series MVP – and this is how he did it. . .

• • •

Following the sweep of the Baltimore Orioles in the ALDS, a champagne-soaked Perez left the Royals clubhouse, took out a broom and danced with fans on top of the dugout. He is allowing fans to be a part of the greatest party in Kansas City since 1985.

"We all want to share this with our fans," Perez said. "We love them. We get energy from them, they are a part of this and we want to party with them."

It seems the only person in the country who doesn't want to party with Perez is Giants reliever Hunter Strickland, who yelled at Perez as he approached home plate in front of Omar Infante's two-run homer in that 2014 World Series Game 2 victory.

"When I got to second after I hit a double," Perez said. "He started to look at me. I got close to home plate, he looked at me. So I asked him, 'What are you looking at me for? I didn't hit a homer. Omar hit a homer.' I don't know what's going on, but forget about that. That's part of the game."

As Strickland began jawing with Perez near home plate, members of the Royals left the dugout and relief ace Greg Holland led a charge of relievers out of the bullpen.

They were sending a message: Don't mess with Sal.

Strickland, who had to be escorted to his dugout by an umpire, was composed back at his locker after the game. He said the whole thing was a "miscommunication" and apologized the next day.

The young reliever said Perez said something in Spanish that he didn't understand, so he said something back.

"I'm not going to back down from anything," Strickland said. "I thought he must have thought I said something to him so, and like I said, it was just the way it is. I got caught up in it."

It will likely be just a blip on the World Series radar screen, but the support Perez's teammates showed when he was challenged proves one thing – this isn't just a team, it's a family.

And families take care of each other.

"We are like a family," Hosmer said. "We have Sal's back."

And when this Series comes to a conclusion, win or lose, you can bet Perez will give Cain a hug, dance with the fans and give everyone a reason to smile.

• • •

Fast forward to 2015, and another World Series Media Day. All the players are sitting at individual tables – with the exception of Cain and Perez. Their tables are placed next to each other, which creates the greatest media moments since their stand-up routine in 2014.

"I don't like the guy, I really don't," said Cain, trying to keep a straight face while Perez blows kisses in his direction. "Do you see what I have to deal with? And I have to deal with this every day."

A collection of Perez's best tweets – involving Cain and a few other teammates – is a viral sensation as the best catcher on the planet chases the all-star center fielder through the clubhouse, airports, training rooms and restaurants.

"I can't catch a break," moaned Cain, as Perez could be heard cooing, "Who loves Salvy?"

"See what I mean? Man, it's a good thing I do love the guy. We all love Salvy. There! I said it! We all love Salvy! Now get that cell phone out of my face!"

What you see with Salvador Perez is what you get. When he's away from the game he dominates, he has as much fun as anyone alive. But when it comes time to get the job done, no one is tougher. During his postseason run to the 2015 World Series MVP Award, he was hit by a swinging bat on the back of his bare hand, he took countless foul balls off his mask and several foul balls struck near the top of his chest protector where there is little padding.

"All part of the game," Perez said. "Now, let's talk about having fun! You know from being a part of that team, from playing with these guys for a long time, like Hosmer, Mike Moustakas, (Jerrod) Dyson, Lorenzo Cain, (Danny) Duffy, you know. Young guys, we're coming from the minor leagues to Kansas City. Being around here for the last six years, we feel comfortable you know. We feel like a family here. And you know, the best thing I can do on the team, I like to do, is make my teammates happy. You know, be happy. Enjoy the game. Play hard. But have fun, too. It's a game, you know. And that's what I like to do. And when I'm behind the home plate I play hard for them."

There's a saying that filters through the Royals clubhouse – if you don't have a selfie with Perez, it must be because you don't want one. The man loves to have fun, but of equal importance, he wants Royals fans to share in the fun.

"This time in Kansas City, it's amazing, man. The fans make me play hard for them, you know what I mean? So every time we come to the field, every time we see the stadium, it's so loud. We know the passion they have. We know all the signs they wave. We look for them – 'Sal for Perez-ident,' 'We Love Salvy' – that's my favorite. It's unbelievable. And I think everything started last year, in the playoffs, when we win the Wild Card game. You know, I see a lot of people happy. See a lot of families happy. You know, that is why the team cares about our fans because they care about us. I like to care, too."

In a Wild Card game that to this day defies logic, Perez was the hero. He drove in Christian Colon with the game-winning run and set the stage for a return to the World Series.

"Whew! That Wild Card game – oh man. When you're down 7-3 to Jon Lester, and we know how important that game is. We have to win it or our season is over. And what I always tell my guys, 'The game is not over.' The game has to be 27 outs to be over, okay. I don't care if we (are) in the ninth, the eighth inning and we are down 20 runs. We can do it. Earn 20 runs. We can make 20 runs, like they do it. And you know, that's what these guys do. And they start to hit some balls pretty good, a base hit, a stolen bag. We get a little opportunity. We (are) close, close. We tie the game in the ninth. You know, Hosmer gets a triple, Christian Colon in the 12th brings Hosmer and I got the big hit. You know, and that is what is important. Play hard to the last out. We learned, you never know what is going to happen. I was 0-for-5 before I got that hit. Oh yeah, every at bat. You want to look for something out over the plate, you know. And they told me, I think, a pretty good curveball. When I see the video after the game, that's a pretty good curveball. And I got a good swing and I hit the ball pretty good, too. After I got that hit, you know, a lot of things come into my mind. And the first thing that I say to, to Hosmer when he got me, when he hugged me, is: 'Papi, we win! Papi we win! Papi we win!' That is what I was about, 'Papi we win!' And he's like, 'I know' and I'm in his face, 'I love you!' That was, that was the best game I played in my life, (until the 2015 World Series).

"So we win, and I want to share it with the fans. I want to share that unbelievable moment. That moment in life that we will never forget – never forget in my life. You know, and what I say we just play hard for the fans.

Play hard for the Kansas City Royals. For the guys in the outfield. For the guys in the infield. For the guys in the bullpen. We know they are doing a tremendous job. So, that made me feel so happy."

And a young team with no postseason success went out and won seven more postseason games in a row and reached the first World Series in Kansas City in 29 years.

"I think that the emotion, the passion, you know, nobody thinks Kansas City can be that for last year. So you got all the little things everybody just made. And we just, think about it, we are doing something special and we get to hear (veteran player) Raul Ibanez. Raul Ibanez he doing some tremendous meeting before every game in the playoffs. It's unbelievable what that guy says. All the things I learned from him. Play hard no matter what. We don't know if we'll never win. If we'll be in that situation again in your life. I know too many people who play for 20 years and be here 20 years and they never made the playoffs. You know, so all the little things, we got to be ready before the game. So every time, every time before the game starts, we play like (it's) the last game of our lives. Like we play the last game of my life. And I think everybody plays that way, too. Hosmer, Alcides...everybody! Moose. Everybody! Alex Gordon makes some nice plays in the left field. Lorenzo Cain, you know, he's unbelievable for last year."

When asked about the Wild Card game victory, Gordon said, "There was nobody I wanted up more in that situation than Sal because I could just see the determination written on his face."

"Ah, ha ha! In the Wild Card game? Yeah, yeah, yeah, I know," Perez said, trembling with energy and excitement. "We never put our heads down. You know, never. Not in the moment, not in the dugout. Every time we make the three out we just come in here, 'We can do it! We can do it! Let's go!' We got in the seventh inning, before we hit in the seventh inning. We go everybody downstairs. We got a quick meeting. Hey guys, that game is over when they make the 27th out, okay. So Ibanez talked for a little bit. And we can do it. And don't want to see nobody with their heads down. Let's go and enjoy the last two innings. Okay?

"We don't (think) like, okay, this guy can beat us. Okay. They are coming to beat us. I think, I think (other teams) have too many confidence, too many confidence. Other things gonna happen that game. You never think that this team is going to beat you, (but they're) going to beat you one day. That's why we play hard every game, no matter what team is coming. If we have to make a hundred runs a game, we going to make hundred runs. You know. The biggest thing, the biggest thing is to win the game. (We are) going to do the best we can do to win the game."

The Royals win the Wild Card game. Then they sweep the hottest team in the American League in the Los Angeles Angels. Then, all that stands between them and the World Series are the Baltimore Orioles.

"The key to our wins was our pitching. The starting pitcher doing their, their job. They hold the game. We win two game in extra innings 2-1, you know 3-2. That's tremendous. That should do it…and with the help of God, and because nothing, nothing gonna happen if we wouldn't have got God. They have a lot too, and we enjoy it. And we know, we never been in playoffs, that team. We wait 29 years to be in the playoff. And the only thing I had in my mind, the only thing we have, of that game in playoffs last year. It's like, we never been here. We have to be happy to be in that situation. We have

Photo Courtesy Peter G. Aiken-USA TODAY Sports

Sep 30, 2014; Kansas City, MO, USA; Kansas City Royals catcher Salvador Perez hits a walk-off single against the Oakland Athletics during the 12th inning of the 2014 American League Wild Card playoff baseball game at Kauffman Stadium. The Royals won 9-8, and began their streak of eight consecutive postseason victories. Many among the Royals mark this as a significant moment in the team's growth, which enabled them to ultimately claim the World Series championship in 2015.

to be happy to be in that game tonight. So we struggling to play the game. Enjoy the game. And you know, play to win."

The man so many fans and players say was responsible for teaching the 2014 Royals how to win was starting pitcher James Shields. Perez agreed.

The starting pitching was dominant in 2014. In 2015, it simply had to get to the fifth or sixth inning, because then the most feared bullpen in the big leagues took over the game.

"Oh, our bullpen, it's unbelievable," Perez said, nodding. "I want my starting pitcher to go to the sixth. If we lead by one run, the game's over. Seriously, that's what I feel like here. No matter what team we play. I just want to do everything we can do to get it to the sixth, seventh inning winning. If we're winning, it's over. We got one of the best bullpens in the league. And the confidence they have. I don't care who's coming. I don't care who's hitting. I don't care if it's Miggy (Miguel Cabrera), I don't care if it's (Mike) Trout. I don't care if it's (Albert) Pujols. Alex Rodriguez.

"When you've got pitchers like that following you with the stuff that they have. With the radar: Kelvin (Herrera) 100 (miles per hour), Wade Davis 97, Greg Holland 97. It's like, it's cool. It's easy, it's easy to do. Catching, catching is the best with those guys. People ask me if Wade is mean. He looks mean? Nah, he's a really good guy. He's timid too. He's a little quiet, a little quiet. But every time he's on the mound, he wants to do the best he can do. And you can see it in his face. You can see it when he competes. You can see that, when he's coming (in) to pitch the game a close game, you know, a close situation game. He's one of the best guys I catch in my career.

"And Kelvin, that's easy. And I know sometimes (what) people (say) when we throw inside and it was close to him. A lot of players 'Hey, don't come in. Hey he throws hard.' We, we're not trying to hit nobody. If I see your reports, like your report, and you cannot hit a fastball inside, I'm going to throw you inside all day. I don't care... if we hit you, we hit you. We're not trying to hit you. We try to pitch you hard. A guy like him, 100, 99, a 101. The change up, 88, 90 mph change up. It's easy to catch him, too. It's easy to catch all my pitchers in the bullpen. I love them all."

The past three years Perez has been a member of the American League All-Star team. In 2014 and 2015 the AL squad won the game, earning the

Royals home field in the World Series.

"Oh, it's unbelievable being in an All-Star Game," he said. "It's amazing for me. Now when I go out and do my best. And when I start to think about it, I think about my past, you know, like all the things I do to get here. I just try to find the moments and I try to win here. You know. But every day is important to me. And when I hear some people say, 'Hey Salvy, you're one of the best catchers,' it's hard to me to believe that. You know, you try to be humble and you don't want nobody to think that Salvador is trying to be mean to me because he's one of the best catchers. I realize that. It's more, it's more impressive when you see a guy like Mariano Rivera."

After catching him during the legendary Yankee closer's swan song, Perez was pulled aside by Rivera for a moment. He told the burly catcher, still in the infancy of his career, that one day, with just a little more seasoning, he was going to be truly great.

"That's amazing when you hear that from Mariano Rivera," he said. "It's great. It means a lot to me. Then the second (All-Star Game), in Minnesota. Derek Jeter, he said, I'll never forget. 'Always be humble.' Always, you know. Always be humble. Respect the game. If you respect the game, the game will respect you. You know, things like that, that's amazing to me. And I will never forget a moment like that in my life. That, it helped me, too. It helped me, too, in my career. It helped me, too, in the field, it helped me, too, off the field too. You know, and that's important, too. Be the same kind of person, on the field and off the field. Those are the things I remember."

The 2014 Royals caught many opponents by surprise. That was not the case in 2015 when they entered spring training with one goal – to win this World Series.

"I expected like that," Perez said, simply. "Well, see, when I get to see… when I start to see Hosmer, Moose. I see this. Gordo. We signed Rios. We got Volquez. And everybody, we talk everyday in the clubhouse. That we need to win the last game. The last game we lose last year. So everybody has talent, has human talent, you know. Every, every, everybody in the clubhouse, know they want to be again in the World Series, they want to be in the playoffs, they want to win the game we lose last year. The last game we lose at home. We want to win this year. So, and I know people didn't believe in the Royals this year, too, but we just, we don't care what team is coming to The K. We will play. We will play (until) the last game in the World Series and we will play hard. We will enjoy the game. And we will try to do the best we can do to win the game.

"When I was 16 back home, I could not dream that big. Nooo! Never! If I said yes, I'm lying to you. Never. No. I, when I signed, I don't think it was going to be this hard. Because it's not easy like people think outside. It's hard to win here. That's why we have to work good in the game and play hard. Because we never know when it can all come to an end."

When fans think of Perez, clutch hitting, toughness, a strong arm, and a big smile immediately come to mind. So do his famous post-game dunks.

"People wonder, 'Who's Salvy going to get?' Yeah! I know what you are talking about," he said, laughing. "I just start to, every night we win. I go sign autographs at a store and I start to sign the bucket and they want me to sign it and do it for charity. I don't know, something like that. You know, like I say, I'm the kinda guy, I like to be happy. I like to joke around. I like to play with my team, you know. I want them laughing. When we are losing, it's real hard. Sometimes too quiet, you know. I just play music. I solve it. Okay, tomorrow is another day. Okay, they beat us today, we'll be ahead tomorrow. Okay?

"That's just a lot of guys helping me. One guy helped me a lot, with my attitude and everything. Yadier Molina. When I was like young, 16, 17 years old. I always follow him. I follow him and I follow Victor Martinez. And you know, two or three years ago, my first opportunity to say to Yadi, and he come into here and I tell him, 'I don't know how it is going to sound, what I got say to you, you are my favorite player.' And he turned around to me and tell to me, 'Hey, thank you. You are the first big league player to tell me that.' Yeah, so he helped me, too.

"Every year, I learn," Perez said. "Every year. I want to get better and better every year. And I want my dunks to get better every year. At first the guys run away. Now, nobody moves now. Nobody moves. I'm doing some magic. They think every time Salvador dumps water, we win. So nobody move, okay. They did the cool water for a little bit. A little bit, nothing going to happen to you except it mean you best player that night. You are a winner – Salvy likes to dunk winners!"

CHAPTER 5

"Thank You, Zack Greinke!"

Shortstop Alcides Escobar was sitting at his locker, going through his usual pre-game routine when a comment from a visitor brought a smile to his face.

"Did you change in a phone booth before tonight's game?" the visitor asked after Escobar had another memorable defensive game. "You play like Superman."

The Royals already have a "Moose," "The Hammer," and "The Wizard of Hoz," why not add Superman to the roster?

"We don't need to add Superman," joked manager Ned Yost. "We have him at shortstop."

When Escobar arrived in Kansas City back in 2010, no one was talking about Superman, Metropolis or the playoffs. All the Royals, Yost and general manager Dayton Moore wanted to do was help turn a once-proud franchise into a contender. When they traded Cy Young Award winner Zack Greinke to Milwaukee for two young players the Royals craved – Escobar and Lorenzo Cain – the process took a major upswing.

When Escobar and Cain arrived in Kansas City, the team was at the bottom rung of the ladder. They were…bad. If they were a high school football team, they would be every team's homecoming opponent, a guaranteed win. But Escobar was thrilled with the trade because Moore promised him that he was a key piece to a playoff puzzle.

"Yeah, when I came here in 2011, I felt like something good was going to happen," Escobar said, as he sat by his locker and watched his teammates come and go to the field and the training room. "I didn't know when because we were in last place. But each year got a little better. After that, in 2012, a little bit better. 2013 a little bit better. In 2014, the best year I have, we go to the World Series. It was a beautiful experience. Everybody's crazy in that moment. And right now we play like, so good. First place, the first division championship in 30 years. We're not the same team I was traded to. We are still the Royals, but now we are champions of the American League."

The accomplishments may line up – mostly – between the 2014 and 2015 Kansas City Royals, but in Escobar's mind the 2015 accomplishments were more impressive, and not just because they won the World Series.

"We might have caught some people by surprise last year," he explained. "This year, we have won a lot of games. And I think we did not get respect early because no one thought we would do it again. But you know, this year is a really good year because everybody wants to do better than last year. Last year we go to the playoffs and the Wild Card. And that's what everybody in this room wants. Every time we play, we want our fans and who we are playing to know that we are playing to win. We are not just showing up, we are out there to win."

Playing to win. That is Escobar's theme, his mantra. He and his teammates are experiencing something new, and they are enjoying this newfound success. It is more fun to go eat in a restaurant and have fans come by your table and thank you for what you and your team mean to the community. It is enjoyable to ride to the ballpark, eager to see your teammates and hear the thunderous home ovation night after night.

And it all began with one, crazy 12-inning game that personified what this team meant to the city, its fans and every member of the reigning World Series champions.

"We played hard last year, and could have won the Central Division, but we lost a game to Detroit, that meant we had to play the Wild Card game," Escobar said. "Man, how crazy is it that your entire season comes (down) to one game? But that was the special moment last year. You know, nobody thought on this team we'd go to the World Series when the season started. We just wanted to be good. We wanted more wins than the year before – when we had a winning season. But that Wildcard Game, that was the best game I play in my life, you know. Like everyone talks about, we're down 7-3 and Lester is on the mound in the seventh inning. That's not easy to beat that guy in that situation. And we come back from (that deficit) and take that game and win that game like that in extra innings. The team is like, we're not going to lose this game. Everybody stay together. We talk about winning in the dugout. No one is just sitting, we're talking, we're yelling for the guys at the plate. It's unbelievable game. You know, when Oakland, they take the lead and go up by four runs and we make three outs and are coming back to the dugout, everybody say, 'Come on! Come on! We can do this!'"

"Oh, that crowd," he continued, excitement evident in his voice. "I can still hear that crowd. And everybody wants to know, was there a cheerleader on our team? Everybody was a cheerleader. Everybody go like, 'Keep pushing. Keep pushing.' Everybody say like, 'We can win! We can win this game.' And when all guys playing together, all guys play with heart, that's the difference. When every guy is playing for just himself, you don't win that game. We had every guy play for the guy next to him in the dugout, next to him in the field. I get excited just talking about it. It is different when you play for each other and the 40,000 fans who are cheering for you."

The clock struck midnight on the 2014 Kansas City Royals' postseason Cinderella story in Game 7 of the World Series. But Escobar didn't want to reflect on last season. Not when the Royals accomplished so much in 2015; not to mention the accolades he earned personally – including a trip to the All-Star Game.

"As a little boy in Venezuela, I could not dream big enough to think about a World Series," he said. "I dream about the big leagues, but not a World Series.

"But there were dreams – I dream of a Gold Glove. I really did – I want to win a Gold Glove (a feat Escobar accomplished Nov. 10, when the 2015 Gold Glove winners were announced). And I dream of an All-Star Game appearance. And I get in the big leagues and Derek Jeter is the All-Star Game shortstop and you know he is going to be the shortstop for a long time. He is 'The Captain.' When you talk about Derek Jeter, you talk about 'The Captain,' and I knew I would not be a starter on an All-Star Game. I have so much respect for that guy. He was the player I want to be. I want to be respected like that. He is my hero in baseball. He started the All-Star Game in 2014 – his last season in baseball – and I start in 2015, the year after he retires. He's gone and I am the first one to start an All-Star Game after he retires and that is just unbelievable to me – unbelievable. I am starting the All-Star Game. Wow, unbelievable. And it was a beautiful experience over there, you know. All my family was over there in Cincinnati – my wife, my son, you know. And I see all the fans, all my teammates, when I go out in the first inning, I say, 'Wow, this is unbelievable!' And the fun thing about an All-Star Game is you get to meet the players you play against for all those years. I look around the locker room, the dugout, and there are all the superstars. I say, 'Wow! There is Albert Pujols. There is Mike Trout.' Those are the guys we played against in the playoffs, and now, they are my teammates, and I am so happy. Here I am, in Cincinnati, on the All-Star team. I am so happy."

Kansas City Royals fans could watch the All-Star Game from Cincinnati and basically watch the Royals starting lineup as the game featured Escobar, third baseman Mike Moustakas, center fielder Lorenzo Cain, catcher Salvador Perez, left fielder Alex Gordon (who missed the game for the second year in a row with an injury), relievers Wade Davis and Kelvin Herrera, and manager Ned Yost and his staff.

"Sharing the game with my family really made it special," Escobar said. "And you could say that sharing it with my Royals family made it even more special. Six of my teammates, seven guys from the same team. And Ned the manager. That was really good. And that's special man, for this organization, all the Kansas City fans. You know that's a special moment. And I think it proved that my opponents and baseball fans finally thought of me as a complete player."

The perception of Escobar as a defensive wizard without much at the plate is one he has fought since he became an every day starter. And it's true, he probably won't win a Silver Slugger award, but he's become much better at the plate than most probably realize. In fact, one of the major talking points during the playoffs – into the World Series – was Escobar's unconventionally aggressive approach in the leadoff spot.

It's not that Esky disagrees a leadoff hitter needs to get on base. He just thinks he should do it by getting a hit, putting wood on the ball. Not necessarily by walking or bunting or any other method that requires the one thing he doesn't have much of:

Patience.

"When Gordo (Alex Gordon) went down with the injury and Ned talks to me about hitting leadoff I say, 'Yes, I can do it,'" Escobar said. "Then Ned gives me the confidence and I hit well and we win a lot of games. I want to be on base so the batters (behind me in the lineup) can hit me in. I hit leadoff in the playoffs and World Series and I do a good job and I am proud. Some say I am too aggressive. You know I don't try to change when I got over there (to hit leadoff). I just try to be aggressive. Basically see the ball, right there in the strike zone, I swing (at) the ball. Sometimes like, a lot of leadoffs, they take the first strike. They take like three, four, five, six pitches. You know for me, I like to swing the bat! This is what I try so, I talk to Ned. If it's in the strike zone, I'm going to swing the bat. He's like, 'You go Esky. You do a really good job.' They trust a lot in me. I like that."

Nov 1, 2015; New York City, NY, USA; Kansas City Royals shortstop Alcides Escobar hits a RBI double against the New York Mets in the 12th inning in Game 5 of the World Series at Citi Field. Typically known more for his spectacular glove work in the field, Escobar was a terror at the plate during the 2015 postseason, jumping on pitches early and often en route to the ALCS MVP award.

Trust is the foundation this team is built upon. Escobar had a great deal of trust and respect for Yost when they were both part of the Milwaukee franchise before Yost took over as the manager of the Royals and made the trade for the man many consider to be the best shortstop in the American League. When Escobar talks about the Royals, trust and fun are two words that pepper the conversation.

"Oh man, I'm having, you know so, so, so, so, so, so, so much fun," he said. "With Ned, I love that guy. For me, when Ned brought me over here to the Royals, that was a really special moment. When he brought me here my first year, I was in spring training, and Ned told me, 'You're here. I'm here. You play for me. When I am here for five years, six years, seven years, here, you play for me those years here.' That was so special. While Ned is here, I am here. Wow! What confidence. I would do anything for that man."

Escobar is a team player. But there are those Superman moments when he somehow manages to hide the large red "S" on his chest and the crimson cape and make the play that makes his teammates and fans gasp. Once such play came during the 2015 season, when he and Omar Infante teamed to rob Cleveland's Roberto Perez of a sure base hit in a 2-1 Royals win at Cleveland.

When the Royals returned home, Moustakas was asked about the play and he simply said, "Filthy, the sickest play I have seen!"

Infante grabbed the hot grounder near second, flipped the ball from his glove to Escobar who grabbed it bare handed. He then did a 360 and fired a perfect strike to Hosmer at first base. "I saw it," Hosmer said. "I was a part of it, and I still don't believe it."

So, what was it like to make that play?

"Yeah! Yeah, that was a really good play when I made with Omar, and got the out on Perez," said a beaming Escobar. "You know, I make a lot of plays, but that one, that's a really special play. Omar flip the ball to me and I got it with my back hand and throw it to first. That's a great play right there. But you know, we have a great middle infield and one of the best center fielders in baseball. Baseball (people) talk about strength up the middle. And I say, 'I got the best infield and the best outfield in the game.' Every night, I go out and if Infante or (Ben) Zobrist play second, we are great. Moose has made great plays at third. Hoz saves everyone errors at first base. Cain in center – the best, he has what I want. So does Hoz. They have Gold Gloves, maybe someday.

"Someday" has arrived, Esky. All-Star. ALCS MVP. Gold Glove shortstop. And World Series Champion.

• • •

Ryleigh Patience was shaking with excitement.

Wearing her brand new Alcides Escobar World Series cap and an Escobar All-Star jersey, the 11-year-old Blackburn (Independence, Mo.) Elementary School fifth-grader was the first person in line among more than 200 who got to meet the ALCS MVP and world champion shortstop.

"I'm so excited," said Ryleigh, a representative of the Make-A-Wish Foundation. "I got to go on the field with Alcides at a game and now, I get to go get my picture taken with him and have him sign my hat."

As a line of fans wrapped completely around the Men's Department at the Independence Center Macy's, Ryleigh and her family stood near the table where Escobar spent two hours signing autographs.

"This is so great, meeting my great fans, like Ryleigh," said a beaming Escobar, as those fans not lucky enough to get an autograph ticket clapped and chanted his name near the front of the store. "We won the World Series in New York, and it is important to me to come back and share with our fans, and this

Independence, Mo. native Ryleigh Patience stands next to her favorite Kansas City Royal, Alcides Escobar, as he signs gear for her. Patience was a representative of the Make-A-Wish Foundation during a signing event at the Independence Center Macy's.

is the best way to do it. I get to meet them, take a photo, sign an autograph and we all have some fun."

No one had more fun than Escobar at the downtown parade and World Series celebration that attracted more than 800,000 fans.

Yes, that figure is correct. Eight. Hundred. Thousand.

"That was the most amazing thing," Escobar said. "I never see that many people in one place. You look out (from the stage in front of Union Station) and all you see are people. So many people. Man, I still can't believe it."

Escobar came up with a gem when he was introduced by his teammate, World Series MVP Salvador Perez.

After thanking the fans, Escobar quipped, "Thank you, Zack Greinke."

The Royals traded Greinke – a Cy Young Award winner – to Milwaukee in 2010. The centerpieces of that trade for the Royals were Escobar and centerfielder Lorenzo Cain – both All-Star players at their respective positions, and both winners of the ALCS MVP award in consecutive seasons.

"Man, one of the best pitchers in the game was traded to Milwaukee for me and Lo, and now, we are world champions – so thank you Royals and thank you Zack Greinke," Escobar said. "I saw today where he declared himself a free agent from the (Los Angeles) Dodgers. He is going to get a lot of money, but we got something better. A world championship for our team and our town."

When asked about all the Royals' late comebacks throughout the postseason – they scored 40 runs from the seventh inning on through extra innings – Escobar just shook his head.

"No matter the score, we always felt like we were going to win," he said. "We got used to the comebacks, we expected them. In that last game, 2-0 going into the top of the ninth (off Mets ace Matt Harvey) we knew we were going to win. I don't know why, but we did."

When asked about his favorite personal moment, he had a quick answer.

"The inside-the-park home run," he said, referring to his first hit in Game 1 off Harvey at Kauffman Stadium. "You don't see many of those. Man, I was tired running the bases but that was special. It was all special."

CHAPTER 6

Cain is Able

October 23, 2015.

It rained, and the Kansas City Royals reigned.

The Boys in Blue were headed back to the World Series for the second year in a row, thanks to a little bit of magic on the base paths by Lorenzo Cain in a 4-3 victory over the Toronto Blue Jays that left the sold-out crowd at Kauffman Stadium breathless.

The same could be said for Cain, too, who somehow managed to score from first base on an eighth-inning single by Eric Hosmer. Cain singled off Blue Jays 20-year-old closer Roberto Osuna, and Hosmer then hit a line drive to right field.

"Mike (Jirschele, third base coach) told us that if the ball is hit to right, and Bautista throws to second, he's sending the runner home," said Cain, who sprinted home from first on the hit. "It's a hustle play and shows that Mike does his homework."

Jirschele, who was criticized for not sending Alex Gordon home in Game 7 of the 2014 World Series as the game ended with him stranded at third base, said, "The minute Lo turned second I was sending him. He's so fast and they need a perfect throw (home) to get him. Lo made me look good tonight."

Then, it was up to Wade Davis, who took over the closer's role after Greg Holland went down late in the season following Tommy John surgery.

Toronto's Russell Martin opened the ninth with a single. Dalton Pompey came in as a pinch runner and stole second and third with no outs. Davis walked Kevin Pillar, then struck out Dioner Navarro and leadoff man Ben

Revere. With runners on second and third and Josh Donaldson at the plate, Davis knew he had to get that final out.

"The last time I pitched after a rain delay, I think, was when I was starting with Tampa Bay and we had a rain delay against Boston," Davis said. "I came out and I don't think I got out of the inning. I just knew I had to get that final out."

Donaldson hit a ground ball to Mike Moustakas at third base and he threw across the diamond to Hosmer, who leaped in the air in celebration. The drama was over and the Royals were American League champions again.

"Moose makes the last out for the second year in a row to send the team to the World Series," Royals legend George Brett said. "When I was playing, I'm saying, 'Hit it to anyone but me.' Moose wanted that ball hit to him."

Cain was happy to share the spotlight with Davis in the ALCS win, as he'd been the center of attention a few weeks earlier when he scored the winning run in the Royals 4-3 win over Seattle that helped them win their first division crown in 30 years.

The young man who didn't pick up a bat and glove until he reached high school garnered national headlines when he was named the MVP of the 2014 ALCS. But his Royals did not win the World Series, and Cain and Co. came back with a vengeance in 2015.

"Last year was so amazing, but I think this year's a better team, personally," Cain said. "We go out and compete each and every night. We try to find a way to win ball games. I think a lot of people were watching us last year wondering what type of team we would put on the field this season. Was last year a fluke, or were we a team that was starting something special – like the Royals back in the 1970s and 80s? Not many people thought we would do what we did last year except the people in this organization. We went out and got it done and we want to do it again and again. Last year was just the start. I knew what kind of team we had in here and like, I feel, just building off last year. The confidence that we gained during the playoffs. Just understanding that a lot of people thought it was a fluke last year. And we just set out to prove people wrong this year. I feel like we did."

In 2014, Cain was a one-man highlight reel during the playoffs, making breath-taking defensive plays and always coming up with the timely hits. When you have a postseason like that, it's hard to select a favorite moment.

"Honestly, I'm like, someone asked me this the other day and I told them I can't just, I can't just point out one moment," he said. "One story. It was so many. There were so many plays being made by everyone. So many diving catches. So many clutch hits. I mean, it was an unbelievable playoffs. That's why I can't just point out one moment. Starting with the Wild Card game. Unbelievable game to be a part of. Then just going into the playoffs, playing the Angels, playing the Orioles. How many guys stepped up and just made plays? And just got it done on the field? And the whole experience of the playoffs, the Wild Card game, the playoffs. Then getting a chance to play in the World Series was something that I just want to, I just want to tell my son once he gets a little older. And now, I can talk to him about winning a World Series."

The relationship between Cain and catcher Salvador Perez has been well documented. Perez loves to harass Cain by chasing him through restaurants, airports and locker rooms with his cell phone running, capturing some of the most talked about selfies – or, maybe they should be called Salvys – on the Internet. So it should come as no surprise that Cain was one of the first to congratulate Perez when he collected the game-winning hit in the 2014 Wild Card game.

Photo Courtesy Matt Nance

Royals All-Star centerfielder Lorenzo Cain smiles and interacts with the crowd during the 2015 World Series victory parade in downtown Kansas City. Known for his wide, infectious grin as well as his penchant for making spectacular plays in the outfield, Cain is yet another young star around whom the organization has built its success.

"I was probably standing on the top step of the dugout when Salvy got the hit," Cain said, "because I'm very close to him. So I was probably on the top step. I was there watching him, definitely watching him and like I said, he stepped up in a big way, too. He's definitely a great guy in here. He's definitely one of our clutch players and stepped up and probably got one of his biggest hits to start our journey into the playoffs."

Following his MVP performance in the ALCS, Cain walked about Kauffman Stadium carrying his newborn son, Cameron.

"Every time I see him or someone says his name, it puts a big smile on my face," Cain said. "Every single time. He brings joy to my heart. I love him to death. I can't wait to see him again after a game here at the stadium or at home after a game. One word definitely doesn't speak for it. So, like I say, I love him a lot. It's going to be awesome to share all this with him someday! Definitely a great feeling. He didn't have a clue what was going on right. It's definitely going to be amazing once he gets a little bit older and understands what he got a chance to be on the field and experience. It's going to be awesome and I can't wait 'til that time comes and say he had a chance to be on the field and walk around and celebrate with my wife and my mom and you know, everyone else involved. It was a great experience for everyone involved."

Royals Hall of Famers Frank White (1980) and George Brett (1985) won the ALCS MVP Award. In 2015, his teammate Alcides Escobar won it. That's some elite company.

"It's definitely been a blessing," Cain said. "Something definitely unexpected. I'm still trying to improve and I've got a lot to learn. I'm still, I feel, young in baseball years. So I'm still trying to improve as a player. But I don't know...MVP. It was something they gave to me and I feel like I went out there and made the plays the best I could to help this team win. It was definitely a nice feeling for me and I will admit that. I'm just trying to continue to go out there and get it done."

Cain shared the special postseason moments with his wife, his son and his No. 1 fan – his mother Patricia – who often worked two or three jobs as the single mother of two boys.

"My mom, she raised me. She did the best that she could with two boys growing up. So it definitely wasn't easy on her. But she found a way get it done.

And like I said, just to share that experience with her. Definitely a blessing. I didn't even think about playing sports when I was real young because we didn't have the money and I didn't want to put an added burden on her. I just went to school, came home, did chores, helped around the house. Um, then once I got into high school, got a little older, and things got a little better. She started working one job so I decided to try out for some type of sport. Not knowing that baseball would turn into this at the time. I tried out for the baseball team wearing my jeans and a collared shirt. I wasn't sure how to hold the bat. She didn't want me playing football, so that's the reason I didn't play football. Quickly got cut from the basketball team, so baseball was the best thing that ever happened to me. I mean, baseball was it. It was the only thing I had left. So I tried out for baseball and the rest is history."

After putting all his focus on baseball, he wound up getting a college scholarship to tiny Tallahassee (FL) Community College.

"My only scholarship offer from any school, so it's crazy, was from TCC," Cain said. "But they gave me the opportunity to go there so it was either TCC or stay home. Ended up going to TCC. Played well. They gave me the chance to play centerfield every single day. Ended up playing well. Got drafted – yeah, got drafted – didn't even know what it meant. I got a call from the Brewers and they said I'd been drafted. I never followed (professional) baseball. I never watched it on TV. So once a scout called me, I didn't know it was Draft Day actually. So when he told me he drafted me in the 17th round I was like I just hung up the phone. I just said thank you and then hung up the phone. Next thing I know, the next day it was all in the papers."

After spending some time in the Milwaukee organization – and having Patricia talk him out of walking away from the game when he was mired in a zero-for 50 slump – he received some unsettling news. He had been traded with Escobar to the Kansas City Royals.

"Once I got traded over here, honestly, I didn't know what to expect," Cain revealed. "Milwaukee drafted me and I was accustomed to that. Used to all the players, I'd made a lot of friends over there in Milwaukee. So once I got over here you know I didn't know what to expect. They welcomed me with open arms. Once I got here, they sent me to AAA that first year. That's when I played with Moose and Hoz, Dyson, all those guys. And we were the best Triple-A team I've been a part of and played on. Of course, we won the championship that year. So that was definitely the best team I've ever been a part of and I knew that this organization was definitely headed in the right direction once I got on the team.

"I mean, sometimes you're forced to grow up. And I think that's the situation we were in. It was either continue to get beat or step up to the plate and go out there and compete. Work together as team and find ways to become a championship team. I feel like that's what we did a great job of, we all stepped up in a huge way. It just wasn't one player on this team that was making the playoffs. Or during the season last year. It was a team effort. As a whole we did a great job of that and I think it definitely carried over to this season and we continued to build off that.

"And last year, it was something that I'm sure anyone in this clubhouse didn't expect for us to get out there and win eight in a row (in the playoffs). But we played some really good teams in the Angels and Orioles, and even the A's. I mean, some very impressive teams and I know a lot of people didn't have us winning any of those games. But I say that's the kind of team that we have. It doesn't matter what team is on the other side of that, in that other dugout. We know that we can go out and compete with them. And we definitely showed it last year and we understand that we can compete with them no matter what; this year and last year helped everyone, I feel. We understand that no matter what the name says, what the name is on the jersey of any player, that we can go out there and compete with them and we can play nine strong innings with them, no problem."

I've never been a part of a team that's this close," Cain continued, marveling. "This feels like we have lived together forever. And it feels like we've known each other forever. This group, you can just look around in here. Everything, everybody's gravitating, relaxed, laid back and enjoying each other. No one's just sitting at their locker just being quiet, off to themselves. It's just, the group's very tight. We all love each other. We all have fun together. We all play hard for each other. I think that's the biggest, biggest thing and I think it's really hard to come by on a professional team.

"And we want to share every moment with our fans. 'Cause we understand it's been a long time, not only for this organization but for this city of Kansas

City as well. So we felt like we had to involve them as much as we could. And that's why we went out and had fun together at parties and getting a chance to, once we won it, be out there on the field and show them how much we appreciate them. So that was a huge thing and I'm glad we were able to do that for them this year, bring the trophy home to Kansas City."

CHAPTER 7

True Grit

With all the success Wade Davis experienced as the Kansas City Royals new closer in 2015, and his dramatic late-inning heroics against the Houston Astros, Toronto Blue Jays and New York Mets, it might be easy for the casual fan to forget "The Hammer."

But that would be an injustice to gritty Greg Holland, the man who made such an impact in 2014 that he was awarded the first-ever Mariano Rivera Award, given to the best reliever in baseball (46 saves in 48 attempts). The Royals ran roughshod over the competition last postseason before reaching their first World Series in 29 years. And Holland was responsible for much of that success, even though he took a little detour – a 2,700 mile flight – to meet his newborn son along the way.

He pitched a scoreless inning in the Royals' 9-8, 12-inning win over Oakland on Sept. 30, 2014, in the wildest Wild Card game ever. Holland then chartered a flight to Asheville, N.C., to share the birth of his first child, Nash Gregory, with his wife, Lacey.

"We had to figure out a way for me to get back to the team out in L.A.," Holland said, as the Royals were ready for their best-of-five ALDS series versus the Angels. "It was kind of hectic trying to do that while you're in the delivery room booking flights and stuff, but we made it work."

He flew out on a chartered flight around 4 p.m. from Asheville to John Wayne Airport in Los Angeles. He was scheduled to arrive around 7 p.m., while the game started at 6 p.m. "Man, there was all kinds of traffic, and the driver did a great job, but I didn't get there until 7 p.m. And by get there, I mean arrive at the stadium.

"I didn't know where to go. I kind of made a few security guards nervous, running up to them with a pack over my shoulder with my ID in my hand, saying, 'I'm a player, I'm a player.' And this one security guard ran with me to the clubhouse. He got me there, but I was a lot later than I wanted to be."

All the while, manager Ned Yost had one thought on his mind.

"Where's Holly," Yost said, grinning. "I'm totally into the game, but I'm wondering where my closer is. He was supposed to be here at 3. Ended up, last I heard, 6. And the game started, and it was like 7. Is Holly here yet?"

He was, and he saved the game that night – which is a story he can't wait to tell his son.

"He actually doesn't remember but he was at most of the games," joked Holland, referring to the very pregnant Lacey attending most home games. "I think it will be fun to be able to talk to him and actually even maybe watch a (2014 postseason) game. Watch a couple of the games on television with him. Of me playing. And let him see all the fun we were having as a team and all that. Be able to share that experience with him. That's the beauty of baseball, is being able to share it with people. But at the time, I was just more concerned with Lacey and her health and Nash's health. It was kind of a whirlwind of emotions. We win a crazy Wild Card game and two hours later I'm on a plane. And then the following day I'm on a plane on the way to Anaheim by myself with a newborn kid back home. It was special, man. The adrenaline got me through it I think. 'Cause I didn't sleep much there for about 70 hours."

Unfortunately he got plenty of sleep this postseason as a torn tendon in his right elbow resulted in surgery that sidelined him for the amazing playoff run to the team's world championship. But he was there sharing every minute with his teammates.

"Man, I missed not being able to pitch at the end (of 2015)," he said. "It's just, you remember being a kid and dream of playing the game and sometimes you can take that for granted so when a crowd gets into it and you're in a tight game you remember that feeling. You're like a little kid out there trying to control your emotions. And I think that's the most fun part of it. You know, that adrenaline rush and everybody yelling and screaming and you're out there. It feels like your hair's on fire, but you're trying to look as calm as possible. I think it's just something the more times you're out there the more times you can practice it and get better at it. Just like learning a new pitch or something like that. You just need those reps. And I remember 2011, one of my first years, Ned was quick to throw me and (Aaron) Crow and (Louis) Coleman and Timmy (Collins) in those tight situations, even though we were young, because he knew the more times he ran us out there in those situations we could get more comfortable with them. And it ended up paying big dividends for us the last couple of years. You're never going to be out there flat-lined on the mound no matter how long you pitch. You tend to learn how to use that adrenaline and energy as a positive instead of as a negative."

While he appeared in the 2014 Wild Card game, he didn't get the save or the win. But he got something more important – the thrill of a lifetime.

"Man, I've been a part of some crazy games but sitting there in the seventh and eighth inning with Jon Lester on the mound, knowing how well he'd done against us as a team in his career, was kind of a daunting task," he said. "But I think it was a right moment for us as a team and as an organization. We finally got to a playoff game and it's been 30 years. Your back's against the wall and you're dead in the water and the boys didn't quit, you know. I think the fans had a lot to do with that to be honest with you. 'Cause it just seemed like there was something in the air. We weren't done. We never felt done, even

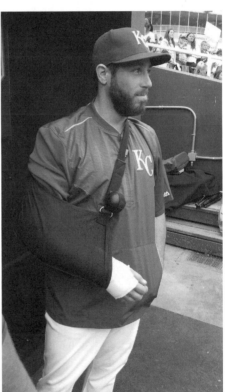

Kansas City Royals closer Greg Holland stayed in good spirits in 2015, though his season was cut short by the increasingly-common Tommy John surgery. The best closer in baseball during the 2014 season, he handed the role to friend and former set-up man Wade Davis for the back end of 2015, and watched proudly as Davis mowed down the competition.

though from the outside looking in it looked that way. You could definitely feel it. I think, like I said, the fans had a lot to do with it. There was just a buzz. We had come too far to worry about losing. We weren't worried about losing at that point. We expected to win until the last out we made. And we could have lost that game. But that doesn't change your mindset as a player when you get in those situations."

And now, a bunch of unproven players were about to make a postseason run for the ages.

"I think that the reason I was able to handle, not the severity, but the importance of the situation was just staying on task. And being in the moment, not worrying about it being a playoff game or the World Series. You know, that being said, once it was all over with it was kind of an influx of emotions. And you know looking back on it in the off season. You're sitting there on the couch. That's when I could really feel some satisfaction for us as a team. And really feel good about what we did and how close we came to winning it.

"And then, we follow up last year with this year – I think it says a lot about the character of our team because I don't think that the experts had us projected to do very well, but that didn't really matter to us. We knew that the people we have in the clubhouse (believed); the ability we have. But that being said, you still want to go out there and prove a point. That it wasn't a fluke. We did that since day one and I think now the boys can make another deep run."

There are so many highs and lows when it comes to relieving, and Holland said he has the right approach to handle any situation.

"You gotta understand that things happen. Some things happen for a reason to build you as a man and a player. I'm going to come back, get healthy and come back stronger than ever and know that fortunately we got a pretty good team without me. I'm looking forward to watching some games. It's gonna sting a little bit. I guess the more games I get to watch the better it will get. With me being out, I am so very proud of Wade. He's a grinder. Just like a lot of those guys down there. They take pride in the day-to-day preparation. And I think a lot of people don't understand that guys like Wade, when you're that good, and Kelvin (Herrera), you don't just show up at 6 p.m. and throw the eighth inning. It's a lot of time and effort. Studying hitters.

Getting in the weight room. Getting your body physically ready every day. That's a grind. And I think that's the coolest part about seeing someone's success is when you see the hours they put in to be as good as they can be. And we have a lot of faith in each other. We are used to knowing who's to your left or who's to your right and stuff like that. It usually meshes well. You see a lot of teams add a bunch of big name free agents and it just doesn't work out sometimes and you can't really tell why. I think the ability to know, to know your teammates well and to have played with them for an extended period of time is a big key in that."

There were no egos in that 2014 bullpen that featured the three-headed monster – H-D-H – Herrera, Davis, Holland.

"It was a lot of fun. They were doing their job in front of me. And that was something we always pride ourselves on was being able to go out there and do what was necessary to win a game. Get the starter the win. The day you didn't have your best stuff you had six guys behind you that are going to pick you up and that was unbelievable. Night in, night out. Trotting Kelvin and Wade out there and seeing what they were doing was incredible to watch. I'm glad I was part of it.

"Actually last year it got to the point where I didn't even watch many of their innings because I was stretching and trying to get loose. I just knew the drill. I knew what was going to happen. So I usually looked at the lineup in the sixth inning and figured out who I was going to face because it was going to be 1, 2, 3 in the seventh, 1, 2, 3 in the eighth. It makes it a lot easier when you can start game planning. It's special watching those guys pitch. It's something you gotta take a step back and admire. A lot of people take that for granted. I mean it's really hard to throw a 1.00 ERA in the major leagues, or any level for that matter. I think sometimes their ability can get taken for granted because they are just so consistent. They are really, really, really good."

So many people think of the iconic image of Holland, a guy who does all he can to avoid the spotlight, grabbing the team flag and carrying it around the Kauffman Stadium field after the team clinched the American League championship, when they look back on the 2014 postseason. The image wound up on the cover of Sports Illustrated and national posters.

"I mean that's not really in my nature to act like that. Yeah, it just was a whirlwind of emotions hit me. You're going to the World Series. A lot of us acted out of character at that point. It was a special moment for all of us. I'm not a very public guy. I'm really not out there that much. I live out in Overland Park and I'm kinda short and stubby so I don't get noticed as much as a guy like Hoz or Gordo. So if somebody does walk up to you and say, 'Hey, good luck tonight,' or something like that it makes you feel good. 'Cause there's a lot of people rooting for you and your team's in a good situation, finally, so that's pretty encouraging."

CHAPTER 8

Señor Smoke

A large, autographed photo of Kelvin Herrera and his Kansas City Royals all-star teammates, triple-matted with commemorative coins from the All-Star Game in Cincinnati, leans against the locker of the young man who has become one of the most feared relievers in baseball.

While he huffs and puffs and sends fastballs exploding toward the plate with speed reaching into the triple-digits on the radar gun, he strikes an intimidating pose. Yet away from the rigors of the mound, setting the stage for Greg Holland or Wade Davis, Herrera is a gentle man whose smile belies his ominous reputation among Major League hitters.

"Last year was special, man," Herrera said. "But I don't have maybe a specific word to describe how I feel about last year, and as a player it was unbelievable. This year and last year, you wake up and the first thing you think about is going to the stadium. The support we receive from the fans. It was unbelievable. I didn't think it would be like that.

Any discussion of the team's success during the past two remarkable seasons always begins at one, specific point.

"We can start, say, talking about the Wild Card game," he said. "That was the game that started everything – the excitement, the playoff (win) streak, the way the fans became a part of our team. Every time we got a base hit or a strikeout the place went nuts. I've never been in atmosphere like that. I hear about NFL games being loud and crazy, but I just see them from the TV. I was in the middle of the Wild Card game and it was so loud. I mean, it was loud and crazy and not like a baseball game. And it was fun, too. Not so much when you are playing because you are just thinking about what you have to do to win, but winning – when Salvy got the hit in the 12th (inning) – the best feeling ever!"

Herrera pitched in the game, but before he took his place on the mound, he watched the fans and the action on the field from both the dugout and the bullpen.

"I wish I had the words, but I don't," he said, shaking his head. "You have the goosebumps. I get them just talking about that game. But, we are professionals, and when we go in to play, we have just one thing on our mind and we have to block out everything else. Players have to field and hit and pitchers have to get the batters out – and even though we were down (7-3 in the bottom of the seventh inning) we found a way to win. And the reason why we win? Well, because we feel like we no gonna give up. We feel like we gonna win the whole game and we get in the seventh inning down by four. We were like, 'We didn't get here to lose. We gonna win.' We just start believing. We started scoring runs, and we tied the ball game.

"You see the Wild Card. It's one game. We play 162 games and we must win the Wild Card to (advance) in the playoffs. We go in one game, anything can happen. If we can get through that first game, we know it's not gonna be that easy, but it will be less pressure for us. The next series was the best out of five. And we get to Anaheim with all the confidence that we know we're gonna win. We knew we were gonna win – we all knew it. When we won the Wild Card game, we were like: 'We can do it! We can do it! We can do it!' That was what happened. We believe in each other."

The bullpen of which he was a part, which earned notoriety with its standout performance during the 2014 postseason and continued to build its legend from all the way through the final out of the 2015 World Series, is something in which Herrera takes great pride. They are a cohesive unit – a family.

"To think about our bullpen – a special group of pitchers," he said, smiling. "I know we been doing our job pretty good. But we don't think about yesterday or think about tomorrow. We think about today. That's why every day we ask each other, "Hey you si or no today? Si! And every time like si! Yes or no and we like Yes! Everyday! That's the question that we ask. Nothing else. Yes or no. And maybe Holland say, Yes! He's always ready – we are all always ready – me in the seventh, Wade in the eighth and Holland in the last inning. That how we do it, and it works."

One of the overlooked qualities of the Royals bullpen is its ability to remain in the moment. They don't get too high or too low – they're always focused on the task at hand.

That doesn't mean it's easy.

"Yeah," Herrera said, shaking his head in agreement. "This is maybe a tougher sport 'cause we play a lot of games and everything that happens, so you can get frustrated with what happened yesterday. But you're going to have a lot more opportunities to fail or to be successful. So you gotta have short memory. And you have to have faith in your catcher and we have faith in Salvy and (backup Drew) Butera. They are so good. We know we can, we can trust them. I don't shake (off a sign), I don't shake either Butera or Salvy. Because they know, they have a good idea how the game is going on. And they know what pitch you can throw and what can work for us. And they know I always like to go with my strength. If we feel like the situation is for a double play, we will figure out what pitch we are gonna throw to get out of the inning or to get out of the tough situation. Or I go for the fastball to get the strikeout – what Drew and Salvy call, I throw."

Photo Courtesy Peter G. Aiken–USA TODAY Sports

Oct 23, 2015; Kansas City, MO, USA; Kansas City Royals relief pitcher Kelvin Herrera follows through on a pitch in the seventh inning against the Toronto Blue Jays in Game 6 of the ALCS at Kauffman Stadium. The cannon strapped to Herrera's right shoulder made him one of the most feared relievers in all of baseball, with his fastball frequently reaching into triple digits.

Unlike some of the early days of baseball when relievers were characters on a team who sported names like Sparky or Goose or the Mad Hungarian, this Royals bullpen is loaded with talent and guys who avoid the spotlight like a vampire hides from the mid-day sun. They don't seek any attention away from the game, because they receive so much when they are on the mound.

"Yeah, we have some funny guys down there – Holland is funny to be around, he is fun," Herrera said. "But we are all just here to do our jobs. I get here and I get ready every single day. Even if they told me I'm done, I get ready because there is a saying, saying like: 'Motivation gets you started, routine gets you going.' This game is about the routine. Because it's a lot of games and you gotta have a good routine to get ready. And I am always ready and Ned knows that. I will come in in any situation. I like to come in at the start of an inning, but if Ned needs me in the middle of the inning – because of my daily routine – I am ready."

And that routine has made Herrera an all-star.

"Ned came over to talk to me and I was not sure why," Herrera explained. "It surprised me a lot because it's not that often that a middle reliever guy is going to the All-Star Game. It's always, has been always the best closer and the best starters. And Wade and I get picked to go – Wade by the players (in the American League) and Ned can pick players and he picks me. Wow! So that was a change. A change. How you say, my perspective of the game changed.

"I never think about being an all star and Ned changed that. Thanks Ned! After he told me, I called my mom. You have to call your mom first, right? And she is back home and doesn't know about an American League and a National League. She just knows I pitch for the Royals and after I told her and my father, explained it to her, she was so happy. I think when she finally knows what happened, she was as happy as me."

For the first time in his young career, Herrera was going to be teammates with the best players in the game – the players he usually battled to help the Royals win.

"Yes. Yes. That was like crazy," he said, laughing. "That is like priceless because you have been around all these superstars. Or players that you face and you want to strike out. Or you want to throw them out and now they are your teammate. Like (Mike) Trout, the Most Valuable Player last year and we play him and (Pujols) in the ALDS last year and now, man, they are my teammates. For one day, I am teammate with Trout and Pujols – a young superstar and one of the best players to ever play the game. And obviously they feel like, this guy strike me out, now he's my teammate. Something like, as soon as we talk in the locker room we became a team. It was unbelievable. And of course the American League won the All-Star Game last year and that gave us homefield advantage in the World Series. We lost in seven, but we had four games here at Kauffman Stadium, and with our fans, that is important – and it is important this year with us being the American League champions. We have homefield through whole playoffs."

Most fans know Herrera for his heat on the mound, but he downplays the importance of making a radar gun the most important measure of his talents.

"If it's strike, it's a good pitch," he explained. "Because it doesn't matter how hard you throw if you don't make the locations. Doesn't matter. I feel like the best pitch is the one that you can control, right? If it's 100 mph and in a good location, that is the best pitch. I like that pitch."

CHAPTER 9

The Terminator

There's a certain…aura attached to the role of the closer in Major League Baseball.

A closer's job is to slam the door on the opposition with the game still technically within their grasp. Closers are usually flamethrowers, or possessed of one particularly exceptional breaking ball able to turn the best hitters in the game into flailing little leaguers. A rare few possess both.

Wade Davis is one of those rarities, and it wasn't until the 2015 season was nearing its grand finale that he became the closer for the Kansas City Royals.

When Greg Holland blew out his elbow in August – and pitched through pain most players could never imagine – he knew on whose shoulders the mantle of closer would eventually settle. And he knew his close friend could handle it.

"When I got the closer's job, I got a nice, big hug from Greg," Davis said.

Formerly a setup man – the middle of the highly-publicized "H-D-H" late innings Royals rotation from the 2014 playoffs – the eighth inning was no longer Davis' primary responsibility. Though, to him, there was little difference between recording three outs in the eighth and three outs in the ninth.

They're all the same to Davis. Each opponent who walks to the plate. Just an out to be checked off the official scorecard.

"The atmosphere might be different, but I approach it same way," Davis said, when asked about his new role as a closer. "The atmosphere makes it easier to have the intensity, the extra oomph…I like to use that energy. I hear the crowd when I come in from the bullpen – our fans are the best – but once the game starts, it's just me, Salvy (catcher Salvador Perez) and the batter."

Davis was unhittable during the Royals' run to their second World Series title. He appeared in eight postseason games and did not allow a run. He picked up four saves and turned in the performance of a lifetime when he stranded runners at second and third with no outs in Game 6 of the American League Championship Series against Toronto.

It was a performance so unbelievable – coming with a 45-minute rain delay sandwiched in between pitches – that Royals legend George Brett declared baseball fans would be talking about it forever.

Just don't expect Davis to be a part of that conversation. He's usually not the talkative type.

"It was a great way to end the game, but that was a team win – everyone contributed," he said. This fits his personality to a "T." Quiet and unassuming, Davis seems more comfortable on the mound in front of 40,000 fans with the game on the line than in front of a microphone. And he'd much rather shift the spotlight to anyone else.

Photo Courtesy Brad Penner-USA TODAY Sports

Nov 1, 2015; New York City, NY, USA; Kansas City Royals relief pitcher Wade Davis throws a pitch against the New York Mets in the 12th inning in Game 5 of the World Series at Citi Field. The right-handed closer was all but unhittable during the 2015 season, and dominated both the playoffs and the World Series.

Still, when the topic of his team arises, even Davis' eyes light up. He's well aware the Royals are something special.

"This year was so different than last year," he said. "We led basically all season, and that was never a problem. We had to win the Wild Card Game last year, and we won eight straight postseason games. This year, we had the same focus and intensity, look at all our come-from-behind wins in the postseason. We were focused from Day 1 of spring training."

He said it is special to be a part of a bullpen that was perhaps the strongest link in the Royals collective chain this season.

"You prepare for what you need to do. You make your pitches, no matter when you're pitching – the eighth or the ninth. There is no mindset. Every inning is the same. No one wants to break the link in the bullpen. I've watched Greg for so long, I follow him. He pitched in sixth, seventh, eighth before he became the closer. We've talked – I know what to do out there."

And he knows that every member of the bullpen checks his ego at the locker room door.

"There are no egos," he said. "We know our roles. Last year it was Kelvin, me and Wade. This year it's Kelvin the eighth and me in the ninth and maybe Hoche (Luke Hochevar) or Ryan (Madson) or even (Danny) Duffy in the seventh. We're links in the chain. The links in the chain. We are all the same. Set it up, close it, keep pushing away. I head to the pen in the third or fourth inning and out there is different than in the dugout. We're not goofing off, but we're pretty relaxed until the fifth or sixth. We always talk, give each other looks, 'Who gets 2-3-4, 3-4-5?' We're different than any other group. Our group is judged on how the bullpen does, not how an individual does. We're proud of what we do. And we're proud of what we did as a team. You see a team win throughout the whole season and it's pretty cool to be on a team that's that dominating. This year was more satisfying because we led most of the season."

While Davis and his teammates feel there is nothing as satisfying as winning a world championship, he believes the foundation for postseason success was established in the 2014 Wild Card game.

"That Wild Card game was crazy," he said. "You felt it as soon as you stepped out on the field. Intense atmosphere, made us a little more comfortable this year because we experienced in that. It gave us the opportunity to play well. Some say it changed us, I don't know if it did. It was a huge transition for us, maybe it did galvanize us as a team, maybe it was a difference maker, but I know that winning that game made a big impact on me and this team. It was historic, and we have a great sense of history because this is a historic sports city and we enjoy sharing our success with our fans."

• • •

In order to do it justice, the stage for this scene has to be set.

Friday, October 23, 2015. Game 6 of the American League Championship Series in Kansas City. Win, and the hometown Royals punch their second consecutive trip to the World Series. Lose, and all the momentum rests with the Toronto Blue Jays for a deciding Game 7.

In the top of the eighth inning, Royals manager Ned Yost had a decision to make. By then, any baseball fan knew of the embarrassment of riches Yost maintained in his bullpen. He had two of his best ready to take the mound – set-up man Ryan Madson and Wade Davis, the premiere closer in the game.

He went with Madson, opting to try to save Davis for the ninth inning and, he hoped, the victory. Unfortunately, Jose Bautista had other plans.

The enigmatic slugger had already blasted a solo homerun that might still be waiting to land earlier in the evening. And after Ben Revere singled, star third baseman Josh Donaldson walked to the plate.

Strikeout.

Now it was Bautista's turn. All he did was turn on a hanging breaking ball, parking it just inside the foul pole in left field and over the wall. With one swing of the bat, Bautista had breathed life back into the Blue Jays, and absolutely deflated the 40,000-plus Royals fans in attendance. A shaken Madson would then walk Edwin Encarnacion, before Yost made his way to the mound and raised his right hand, signaling for Davis. With his usual emotionless precision, the flame-throwing right-hander got Chris Colabello to pop out to second base before striking out Troy Tulowitzki to end the inning...but the damage had been done.

To top it off, a storm rolled through Kansas City, causing a 45-minute rain delay – and the Royals still had to bat. That meant it could be more than an hour before Davis took the mound again; almost assuredly too much time to keep a closer's arm warm. And then there was the little matter of finding a way to generate a run of their own and retake the lead.

Fortunately, the Royals had an ace up their sleeve as well, and its name was Lorenzo Cain.

After Cain led off the bottom half of the frame with a walk, first baseman Eric Hosmer – a veritable RBI machine during the 2015 postseason – punched a single into right field. And that's when Cain's feet erupted in flames.

Not really, of course, but they may as well have for as fast as the All-Star centerfielder was moving. Without so much as a glance at where the ball was headed, Cain put his head down and turned on the jets, racing from first to score – on a single – and give the Royals a 4-3 lead.

Three outs. That's it. That's all that separated the Royals from the World Series, and Wade Davis was pitching. A being whose demeanor on the mound left many only half-jokingly wondering if he was a man or a cyborg. The pennant was in the bag, and the post-game celebration so close the jam-packed stadium could practically taste it in the air.

Now the stage has been set.

This was Davis' moment. A typical reliever couldn't handle it. But, of course, since making the transition to the bullpen in 2014 Davis has been anything but a typical reliever.

"He's the best in the business," said former Royals closer Greg Holland, who turned his ninth inning duties over to Davis permanently following season-ending Tommy John surgery.

During the delay, Davis did all he could to stay warm. He stretched. He applied heat packs to his arm. He played catch with backup catcher Drew Butera in the batting cages hidden within the bowels of Kauffman Stadium. And into his solitude, one memory made itself a most unwelcome guest.

This was not the first time he had been in this situation.

"I did it once before," Davis recalled after the game. "I was a starter for (the Tampa Bay Rays) and we were playing Boston. There was a delay of about 45 minutes or so, and I came back out to pitch."

How did that end up?

"I didn't get out of the inning."

Yost and pitching coach Dave Eiland played out every possible scenario in their heads during the down time. Ultimately, they decided to send Davis back out for the top of the 9th.

"It was a 45-minute delay, but it seemed like four hours," Yost said.

Afterward, Davis was asked if he thought about that game versus the Red Sox before emerging from the dugout with a trip to the World Series hanging in the balance.

"Oh yeah," he said, softly. "I remembered."

Right away, it seemed as if something was off. Russell Martin greeted Davis with a first-pitch single. He was replaced by pinch runner Dalton Pompey, who immediately stole second and third base.

The tying run was on third base, just like that, with no outs.

He then walked Kevin Pillar, who stole second.

Now the tying run was on third base and the go-ahead run on second. Still no outs.

"Not the way I wanted the inning to start," Davis admitted.

"I could tell the delay affected him from (watching up in) my suite," added Kansas City legend, MLB Hall of Famer, and Royals vice president George Brett. "He gives up a hit and a walk to the first two batters – they have second and third and no outs – and I'll be damned if he doesn't pitch out of it."

In fact, if Davis wanted to break a sweat, it didn't show. He just reached deep down and did what he'd done all season long.

He dominated.

The first out was recorded when he blew a 98-mile-per-hour fastball by Dioner Navarro. The second, moments later when he threw a curveball that froze Revere solid.

By this time, the crowd was at a fever pitch. What had looked like a budding disaster had suddenly shifted. No outs with two men on became two outs with two men on, but there was still one, minor detail to wrap up.

That detail being the man striding to the plate. Josh Donaldson. The All-Star. He of the 41 home runs. Arguably the most dangerous hitter in the game.

"For God's sake, he strikes out two batters and then the likely MVP comes up – Donaldson," Brett said. "Hell, I thought I was going to have a heart attack, and I wasn't even playing."

Davis wasn't going to back down. Instead, he challenged Donaldson, throwing four straight fastballs that were little more than a red and white blur as they streaked toward home plate.

Donaldson caught the fourth of these, timing it just right. The crack of the bat cut through the noise of the crowd, and the ball shot away as if out of a cannon.

Right at Royals third baseman Mike Moustakas. As easily as if he were taking pre-game grounders, "Moose" plucked the ball off the ground, pulled it from his glove, and fired a rocket to Hosmer at first.

Game over. The Kansas City Royals were, once again, the champions of the American League, and the celebration began.

"Greatest relief performance, especially given the circumstances, in team history," said Brett, who television cameras had shown checking his pulse in his seat. "I don't know how the hell he did it, I'm just happy he did."

"Wade never shows much emotion," said catcher Salvador Perez, who rushed to the mound to give Davis a bear hug. "But tonight, he throws glove in the air and shows emotion. I like that, I like that a lot."

Long after the game was over, family members joined the team on the field and Davis stood on the mound with the loves of his life - his wife, Katelyn, and their daughter, Sully Rose, who was tucked in his arms. And maybe at two years old she couldn't quite grasp what all the fuss was about, the sheer magnitude of what her dad had just accomplished. But, then, she didn't really need to. She was just happy to see him happy.

"I had to get it done after Lo (Cain) scored from first on Hoz's single," said Davis, who looked less like a Terminator and more like an overjoyed (and maybe even relieved) ballplayer, as Sully Rose showered him with kisses while he attempted to talk. "Besides, I wanted to go back to the World Series."

A slight smile lifted the corner of his mouth.

"I guess I still had a little bit of magic."

CHAPTER 10

Building a Bridge

Ryan Madson has become a bridge builder for the Kansas City Royals, but his tools are a baseball and a glove.

He was the man Ned Yost would hand the ball to, in order to keep the lead safe for Kelvin Herrera, Wade Davis, or Greg Holland - before he was sidelined with an injury. And he was more than anyone could have counted on at the start of the season.

In what turned out to be one of general manager Dayton Moore's most shrewd off-season moves, the Royals signed Madson to a minor-league contract even though he was out of baseball the past three seasons due to Tommy John surgery and other complications. The gamble paid off. Madson became an integral part of the best bullpen in baseball, and is now a world champion.

Not bad for a longshot.

"I'm just trying to get outs when they are needed just like all year long," Madson said, when asked about his role changing from a long-innings guy in blowouts to a bridge guy in the sixth or seventh innings. "Really in my career, that was my focus. That's just what I'm trying to do, is get outs when they are needed. That's it. Let everything else take care of itself.

"To me, there really isn't any difference when I come in," he added, echoing the sentiment of closer Wade Davis. "I don't know. I'm just playing it off my last game. That's how I do for the whole season. You want to get better than your last game. Just do that and get the job done for these guys."

Madson was a member of the Philadelphia Phillies from 2003 to 2011, and said he enjoys the fun of being a member of the Royals.

"Coming from the Philly organization, it's pretty serious over there," he said. "Not a bad thing or a good thing. It's just different. So when you come over here and see that you play the game as hard as you can and then after that, there's nothing else you can do, then just don't pout about it. Don't hang your head. Just keep doing what you're doing. Have fun. Enjoy your teammates. And go out there the next day and try to win. It's a good attribute to have.

"And I love being part of this bullpen. I take a lot of pride in that. You want to be the best bullpen in the league. So to be a part of guys that are out there, it's just amazing. I don't know. Sometimes I just gotta look back and say, 'Wow! I can't believe I'm part of a bullpen like this.' I guess this is the right time, the right spot for me.

"Last year's pen was one of the best groups that I've ever seen come out in the seventh, eighth, and ninth (innings) with Kelvin (Herrera), Wade and Greg (Holland). They were so dominant. It's not that easy, especially that late in the game. And the way they handled it is tremendous. We're just trying to keep up with that kind of theme. You just do what you are going to do. That's why all these players are in here is because you just trust yourself and go out there and play the game. And know that you are meant to be in that spot.

"I wasn't here last year, but I know the playoffs were intense because I was there with Philadelphia. Yeah, every playoff is intense. I don't know how many playoff games I've been in now. It's a handful. And each one of them is exactly the same. You're running at 100-percent. More than that actually. You're over revving at times. As far as focus, physical exertion, and mental approach you have to stay within yourself to get the job done. You have to have confidence in yourself and your teammates and we have extreme confidence in those areas.

"Now, after being out three years, I didn't know if I'd be back to being a part of something like (the postseason). I knew that we were going to be in the playoffs more than likely. With playoffs, comes real strenuous situations. I never looked that far ahead. That's part of a reliever in general, is just going day to day. That's how we survive.

"And it's nice to know your role. And the personalities out there, when I first came here, I couldn't have handpicked a better group of guys, really.

Photo Courtesy Peter G. Aiken-USA TODAY Sports

Apr 17, 2015; Kansas City, MO; Kansas City Royals shortstop Alcides Escobar lays on the ground after getting hurt while attempting to turn a double play. This moment kick-started a series of altercations with opposing teams early in the season, as the Royals sought to protect their own.

Photo Courtesy Peter G. Aiken-USA TODAY Sports

Apr 19, 2015; Kansas City, MO; Oakland Athletics third baseman Brett Lawrie has to be restrained after a 100-mph fastball from Kansas City Royals pitcher Kelvin Herrera buzzed behind his head. Herrera was ejected from the game. This came two days after Lawrie's controversial slide injured Alcides Escobar, and a day after Royals starter Yordano Ventura hit Lawrie with a pitch in apparent retaliation. Ventura was ejected and the benches cleared. The lasting effect, however, may have been to serve notice to the rest of baseball that the Royals were not going to be the overlooked underdogs they were in 2014.

Rapper Fetty Wap, middle in blue t-shirt and Royals cap, is joined by, from left, Lorenzo Cain, Salvador Perez, Jarrod Dyson (kneeling), and Jeremy Guthrie, before a home game during the 2015 season. Cain used Fetty's popular song "Trap Queen" as his walk-up music when coming to the plate, and it eventually became the team's unofficial anthem.

Photo Courtesy Lenny Cohen

Kansas City is known as the "City of Fountains" for a reason – chiefly because there are a great many of them within the metropolitan area. When the Royals advance to the postseason the fountains run blue, just like this one in the Kansas City suburb of Prairie Village, Kan. The additional decorations are an individual touch.

Oct 26, 1985; Kansas City, Mo; Kansas City Royals catcher Jim Sundberg celebrates after pinch hitter Dane Iorg hit the game winner in the bottom of the 9th inning during Game 6 of the 1985 World Series, giving the Royals a 2-1 victory. The pivotal Game 6 was the turning point in the series, as it forced a Game 7 during which an energized Royals club trounced the Cardinals to claim the crown.

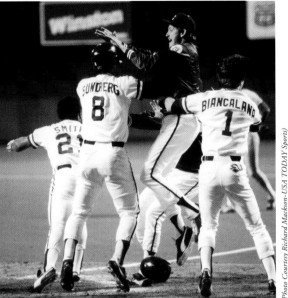

Photo Courtesy Richard Mackson–USA TODAY Sports

Photo Courtesy Richard Mackson–USA TODAY Sports

Oct 27, 1985; Kansas City, MO; Kansas City Royals fans celebrate on the field at Royals Stadium after watching their team defeat the St. Louis Cardinals 11-0 in Game 7 of the 1985 World Series. At the time, fans would never have predicted it would be three decades until the next championship for the Royals, as they were a dominant force in the American League for many years before finally claiming the 1985 title.

As many fans know, Salvador Perez is nothing if not a social media savant. His Instagram account is one of the most popular in Major League Baseball, and for good reason – he's as happy and active off the field as he is on it. His antics featuring close friend Lorenzo Cain have become the stuff of local legend. Here, Perez takes the field at Kauffman Stadium during the 2015 World Series.

Photo Courtesy Salvador Perez Instagram(@salvadorp13)

Photo Courtesy Noah K. Murray–USA TODAY Sports

Oct 31, 2015; New York City, NY; New York Mets second baseman Daniel Murphy commits a fielding error on a ball hit by Kansas City Royals first baseman Eric Hosmer during the 8th inning in Game 4 of the World Series at Citi Field. A big part of what made the Royals so difficult to defeat was their ability to put the ball in play. The Mets defense was shaky, as Murphy in particular made a couple of key errors which opened the door for rallies, including this one – and the Royals never failed to take advantage.

Photo Courtesy Robert Deutsch-USA TODAY Sports

Nov 1, 2015; New York City, NY; Kansas City Royals first baseman Eric Hosmer scores the tying run past New York Mets catcher Travis d'Arnaud in the 9th inning in Game 5 of the World Series at Citi Field. This was perhaps the defining moment of an incredible postseason for the Royals. Hosmer's mad dash from third-base on a fielder's choice ground ball forced the action to a fever pitch. Had first baseman Lucas Duda made a good throw, Hosmer likely would have been tagged out and the series returned to Kansas City. Instead, he forced the action, Duda made a panicked and off-target throw, and the rest is history.

Nov 1, 2015; New York City, NY; New York Mets starting pitcher Matt Harvey is relieved by manager Terry Collins in the 9th inning against the Kansas City Royals in Game 5 of the World Series at Citi Field. This was the conclusion of a situation which was the cause of much debate in the moment, and will continue to be all off-season. Harvey dominated the Royals for eight innings and when Collins planned to remove him for the 9th, he forcefully – and successfully – argued his case to go for the complete game. As they had done all postseason long, the Royals found a way to get it done, plating a run and putting Eric Hosmer on third. He would eventually score on Mike Moustakas' grounder to the Mets' Jeurys Familia to tie the game.

Photo Courtesy Jeff Curry-USA TODAY Sports)

Photo Courtesy Brad Penner-USA TODAY Sports

Nov 1, 2015; New York City, NY; Kansas City Royals pinch hitter Christian Colón hits a RBI single against the New York Mets in the 12th inning in Game 5 of the World Series at Citi Field. The run driven in by Colón's clutch hit proved to be the winning run of the series. Colón is making a career of coming through in the most important situations – he also scored the winning run during the 2014 Wild Card game...in the 12th inning.

Photo Courtesy Brad Penner-USA TODAY Sports

Nov 1, 2015; New York City, NY; Inevitability sinks in among the players and fans of the New York Mets during the 12th inning of Game 5 of the World Series at Citi Field. The Royals made faces such as these common throughout the postseason with their seemingly never-ending onslaught of late-inning comebacks. Featured prominently is Mets pitcher Noah Syndergaard, whose shutdown performance during Game 3 and controversial brushback of Alcides Escobar only fanned the flames of Kansas City's determination.

Photo Courtesy Anthony Gruppuso–USA TODAY Sports

Nov 1, 2015; New York City, NY; Victory. The Kansas City Royals rush the field, spurred on by a surprising number of their fans at Citi Field in New York, after Wade Davis records the final out of the 2015 World Series. The celebration was only beginning, however, and would come to a head when more than 800,000 fans invaded downtown Kansas City for the victory parade.

Photo Courtesy AP Photo/Matt Slocum

Kansas City Royals catcher Salvador Perez dunks manager Ned Yost after claiming the 2015 World Series title with a Game 5 victory over the New York Mets, Sunday, Nov. 1, 2015, in New York. The post-game dousing has become a beloved post-victory tradition in Kansas City, as the boisterous catcher typically soaks the Most Valuable Player of each game. In a way, Yost should feel honored ; Perez himself said he only dunks "winners."

Photo Courtesy AP Photo/David J. Phillip

Another angle on the photo above shows the impact of Salvador Perez's Gatorade jug bath of Manager Ned Yost. Perez selected Yost for the dunking and tracked him across the field, before the grinning manager finally just turned to his catcher and faced the inevitable. A World Series championship and accompanying World Series MVP trophy likely earned Perez the right to some fun in Yost's eyes.

Photo Courtesy Al Bello/Pool Photo via USA TODAY Sports

Nov 1, 2015; New York City, NY; Kansas City Royals manager Ned Yost celebrates with owner David Glass following the presentation of the Commissioners Trophy after defeating the New York Mets in Game 5 of the World Series at Citi Field. Glass was as elated as any of the players, coaches, or fans to hoist the trophy he coveted since purchasing the team in 2000. Despite appreciating the American League Championship trophy of 2014, Glass half-teasingly told general manager Dayton Moore and Yost in 2015 he wanted "the one with the little flags."

Photo Courtesy Al Bello/Pool Photo via USA TODAY Sports

Nov 1, 2015; New York City, NY; Surrounded by Kansas City Royals and Major League Baseball executives on a makeshift stage, Royals catcher Salvador Perez celebrates in the clubhouse after being presented with the 2015 World Series MVP award. This photo encapsulates Perez in a nutshell, whose love for the game keeps him playing year-round, through aches, and pains, and fatigue. He is beloved not just by his teammates, but by the whole of Kansas City.

Photo courtesy of Brad Penner–USA TODAY Sports

Nov 1, 2015; New York City, NY; Kansas City Royals first baseman Eric Hosmer sprays champagne in the clubhouse after defeating the New York Mets to win Game 5 of the 2015 World Series at Citi Field. It was the Royals' third-such champagne celebration of the 2015 postseason, and undoubtedly the sweetest.

Photo Courtesy Jeff Curry–USA TODAY Sports

Nov 1, 2015; New York City, NY; Kansas City Royals players pose for a team photo after defeating the New York Mets in Game 5 of the World Series at Citi Field – earning them the 2015 World Series crown. Throughout the 2014 and 2015 seasons, a major theme to emerge from the Royals' clubhouse has been that of family. The team is a family. And that closeness came to include the thousands upon thousands of Royals fans who showed their love and support. Such a relationship between team and town is rare, but whatever magic it required Kansas City and its Royals had it in spades.

Photo courtesy of Matt Nance

As one might expect, Kansas City Royals catcher and 2015 World Series MVP Salvador Perez was one of the most active and excited participants in the Nov. 3, 2015 victory parade in downtown Kansas City. Joined in the truck by members of his family, Perez slapped high-fives with and spoke to numerous fans along the route.

Photo courtesy of Matt Nance

A giant floating baseball precedes the arrival of the players, coaches, and franchise executives of the 2015 World Series champion Kansas City Royals, during the victory celebration Nov. 3, 2015 in downtown Kansas City. More than 800,000 fans lined the route and the rally site at Union Station to pay one final tribute to their team – a team which captivated an entire nation with its aggressive, resilient style of play.

Kansas City officials were said to expect approximately 250,000 attendees Nov. 3, 2015, at the 2015 World Series victory parade and rally in downtown Kansas City. They underestimated just how much the metropolitan area loved its Royals, as the route was flooded by more than 800,000 people.

Photo Courtesy AP Photo/Reed Hoffmann

Near the 2015 World Series victory parade's final destination of Union Station, children resorted to climbing trees (under the careful supervision of their parents) to see the action. Their enthusiasm was understandable, and it was shared by the adults in attendance as well. Though none of the adults appeared ready to climb trees to gain a better vantage point.

Photo Courtesy Bob Snodgrass

Photo courtesy of Matt Nance

Kansas City Royals first baseman Eric Hosmer enjoys the view from the back of his assigned pickup truck during the World Series celebration and parade Nov 3, 2015 in downtown Kansas City. Members of the team repeatedly indicated how stunned they were by the number of people in attendance – making it fitting that their shirts all bore the slogan "Thank You Kansas City."

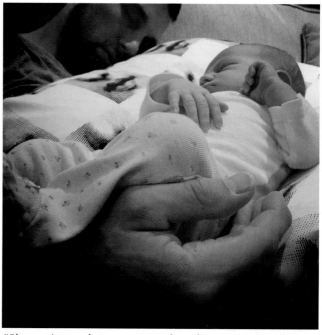

"She won't ever have to worry about having a protector." This photo was taken by Julianna Zobrist, of her newborn daughter, Blaise Royal Zobrist, and her husband, Royals second-baseman Ben Zobrist. Julianna's pregnancy and curiosity over when the baby would arrive became one of the most talked-about storylines of the post-season.

"There are to dos to be done and songs to be written... but then there's this." Another contribution from Julianna Zobrist, this one of her and newborn daughter Blaise. The Zobrist family quickly and completely captured the hearts of Kansas City fans after Ben joined the Royals via trade in late July. The feeling was mutual, as Ben and Julianna both expressed an instant connection with the team, the city, and the fans.

Photo Courtesy Michael McKinley

This photo, taken from the Westin Crown Center Hotel near Union Station, provides another astonishing depiction of just how many people showed up Nov. 3, 2015 to cheer on the Royals one last time. During the 2015 postseason, Kansas City Mayor Sly James became fond of the phrase, "New York is the City that Never Sleeps, but Kansas City is the City that Never Quits." And the fans proved him correct that day, as they seemed to "never quit" arriving – more than 800,000 in all.

Photo Courtesy Mike Swanson/@Swanee54

Photo Courtesy Salvador Perez, Instagram/@salvadorp13

Posted by Kansas City Royals Vice President of Communications and Broadcasting Mike Swanson to his Twitter account, prior to Eric Hosmer and Salvador Perez's Nov. 4 appearance on "The Tonight Show with Jimmy Fallon." NBC sent a jet to pick up the boys, and Perez got to perform his usual post-game water dunk on Jimmy during the program.

Posted by Salvador Perez to his Instagram account, and taken outside their dressing room prior to their appearance on "The Tonight Show with Jimmy Fallon." Perez offered a number of behind the scenes glimpses at the trip to New York City, and millions of viewers tuned in live to catch the show.

You've got funny guys. You've got serious guys. Quiet guys. Loud guys. But nobody's playing for themselves. They're playing for the team. And that's what helps everybody go. You just feed off each other and everybody's rooting for each other and pulling for each other to do well. And that helps out. That's not everywhere. But it's here. And our fans are the best. But to be honest with you, when I come in from the pen, I don't hear anything, really. You could ask everybody. You don't hear it. You're in that zone. You hear it afterwards, but not while you're out there doing your job."

CHAPTER 11

Young at Heart

No one knew what to expect from lanky right-hander Chris Young when the Royals signed him in spring training.

But in a season that featured so much success, on a team with so many recognizable personalities, Young was one of the unsung heroes who contributed everything he had to bringing the World Series trophy back to Kansas City.

"Well, from my first day at spring training it was evident that this team had an expectation to win and get back to where they were last year," the always-genial Young said. "I think everybody was disappointed and motivated to return to the World Series and hopefully win it. And it was so apparent from Day 1. I think I said this before, I called home and told my wife, 'This team truly expects to win.' And it felt different than other camps I've been in, where there was more a hope to win than an expectation. And I think the team lived up to that expectation all season."

It's hard to imagine a pitcher more resilient than Young. One day after finding out his father had died, he was slated to start versus the Cleveland Indians on Sept. 27. Nobody expected him to pitch. Not with the grief so fresh.

Young demanded the ball, threw five innings of no-hit baseball, and got on a plane to Texas to honor his father. That resolve didn't earn him the love and respect of his teammates – he already had that. But it earned him a crucial role as both a reliever and spot starter throughout the 2015 postseason.

Young was given the ball in Game 4 of the World Series, a must-win since his team had stumbled badly in Game 3. And the start was coming on short rest, as he'd thrown three shutout innings in the Royals' remarkable, 5-4, 14-inning victory in Game 1 in Kansas City.

No problem.

"I came in yesterday and got my normal routine in and just treated it as a normal start," Young said. "Like I've said, I'm here to do whatever the team needs, whether that's relieve or start. And my body feels fine; physically, I'm not worried about bouncing back and I'm excited to be out there. And it is special to pitch against my old team (Young was with the Mets from 2011-2012). Well, yeah, no matter who you play in the World Series it's special. It's what every player should play for. It's certainly what I've aspired to participate in my entire career. And, yeah, to do it against a club that I have a lot of friends over there, I have a great respect for their organization. I'm grateful for the opportunity they gave me. And certainly to see them and their success over the last few years, since I last played here, it's great. I'm happy for them. I just hope we find a way to beat them."

Oct 20, 2015; Toronto, Ontario, CAN; Kansas City Royals manager Ned Yost convenes with his infield, including pitcher Chris Young (middle), during the fifth inning of Game 4 of the 2015 American League Championship Series. A spring signing by general manager Dayton Moore, the steady, stoic Young proved an invaluable asset throughout the season both in spot starts and out of the bullpen. His father, Charles Young, died unexpectedly in September – succumbing to a battle with cancer. The team rallied around him, and Young responded, giving the Royals inning after inning of outstanding pitching throughout the postseason.

Photo Courtesy John E. Sokolowski-USA TODAY Sports

They did, and Young was once again solid. He threw four innings of two-hit baseball before turning the ball over to the bullpen. The Royals would go on to take the game 5-3.

If anything, his Game 1 victory out of the pen and Ryan Madson's win in Game 4 – Young came away with a no-decision – proved to him how team-oriented the Royals really were.

"I don't really get caught up in the statistics," he said. "There are a number of pitchers that deserved to win in that game the other night. I just happened to get it. Individual wins and losses are somewhat - I don't know - it's crazy for me to think that a pitcher gets an individual win and loss. When the Cleveland Cavaliers win a game, LeBron James doesn't get the win. Tony Romo doesn't get it for the Dallas Cowboys; it's the team. Baseball is the same way. It's a team sport. It's an individual team sport but collectively it takes everybody to win these games. So I don't really look at it -- I'm just happy to be part of a great team, a winning team and for the opportunity they've given me. And all the statistics, maybe one day I'll look back on it and appreciate it. But if a win was defined a different way 150 years ago, I probably wouldn't have had it."

Though Young is known as a control pitcher and not for his velocity, manager Ned Yost and many members of the media covering the series marveled at the way his velocity skyrocketed during his relief appearance in Game 1. But when asked about it, Young just shrugged his shoulders.

"Oh, I don't know if there's one specific answer," he said. "And I don't know if I know the answer to that. I just know that physically I feel good. I can say from a physical and mental standpoint I prepare and I put in the work, I put in the effort. Last year when the season ended I was extremely disappointed with the ending of the season, and I went home and I got to work immediately. I said this isn't going to happen again. Two bad starts last September and I felt like it hurt our team's chances in Seattle of making the playoffs, and that motivated me all offseason. And maybe that's why.

"Maybe it's the extra training. It was the first offseason in a while where I was able to actually train and not rehab, per se. And so maybe - there are probably a lot of combinations that are in play here that I can attribute to that. But ultimately I think some of it is just the adrenaline of pitching for something that I've strived to do my entire life. When you get in that situation the emotion, the adrenaline and everything, you know, it takes you to maybe levels you haven't seen in a while."

Young is now far away from the neon lights of Broadway, but when he started for the Mets, he believed the team had a bright future.

"When I was here I thought we had good teams. I enjoyed my time here. I really liked it. I love the city. I love the fans. I love the organization. And I thought that the team was going the right direction. You could sense that there was a group of guys that really wanted to win. And there was some development that needed to take place. And certainly that has happened. And with the horses they have in the rotation and the pieces offensively, it's why they are here in the World Series. And it's extremely impressive. They're a great club, and I'm extremely happy for them.

"But now, I'm a member of the Royals. It's like you said, once you win a championship, it's a part of history. As I said, I think every player strives to be part of a championship club. For me to have this opportunity here, with the group of guys that really embody, in my mind, everything a team should be, completely selfless and care only about winning. They don't care how they get it done; they just want to win. To be part of that it's so special for me. It's everything that I could play for. And I'm just beyond grateful for the opportunity the Royals have given me.

"It's special – to be on this team and start Game 4 – but I don't get caught up in the individual significance. It's more about the team for me. To be part of a winning team and contribute to a win, whether that's pitching in relief or starting, not pitching at all, whatever this team needs me to do. If I can help them win, that's what I'm here to do. And to bridge the two questions together, it's about a championship, and that's the ultimate goal. It's the ultimate goal for everybody in that clubhouse for us. So I think each and every person in there would sacrifice whatever they need to do for the team. And so it's just - I can't really describe the feeling of it. It's just there. And everybody knows what's the most important - what the most important goal is, and that's the team."

CHAPTER 12

"That's What Speed Do"

Jarrod Dyson became a household name in Kansas City following the 2014 postseason run in which he ran wild over the Oakland A's, Los Angeles Angels, Baltimore Orioles, and San Francisco Giants.

Although not an everyday player, he made the most of his time on the field – especially on the base paths, where his thefts ranked up there with the James Gang, Bonnie and Clyde, and John Dillinger.

"Dice had so many thefts, I expected to see his poster in a post office," joked his good friend and teammate Eric Hosmer. "When Dice comes into a game, you know what he's going to do – and that's tough. Everyone in the park knows he's in there to steal a base and he still goes out and does it."

After stealing a base, Dyson would turn to his teammates in the dugout and make a motion like he was revving the engine of a motorcycle. When former Royals designated hitter Billy

Photo Courtesy Bob Snodgrass

Kansas City Royals outfielder Jarrod Dyson poses with a pair of young fans at a signing event. The speed demon is a fan favorite in Kansas City, known almost as well for coining the phrase "That's what speed do" during the 2014 postseason as he is for terrorizing opposing catchers on the basepaths.

Butler stole a 2014 postseason base, he imitated Dyson, much to the delight of the diminutive base thief.

When asked about his importance to the Royals 2014 playoff run, Dyson simply said, "That's what speed do."

That became the catchphrase of the entire playoffs. The quote was seen on billboards, t-shirts and posters. It made Dyson an important part of a special season and Kansas City sports lore.

"That, that was all crazy," Dyson said, when asked about 2014 and the playoffs. "Sometimes you think that, because you are living your dream out, when you see a quote that you made and it blows up in Kansas City, it makes you feel special. Like you really did something for the city, or you're doing something that they love. I take a lot of pride in that and I love that the fans cheer me on every time that I take the field. By me being a backup I go out there and give it my all for Kansas City, and I'm going to continue to do that as long as I'm on the field."

No one on the team has more desire or heart than Dyson, who has been told he couldn't make it so many times, that he just laughs at the number of rejections he received before making it to the big leagues.

"I think that a lot of the drive has to do with my background. It has a lot to do with me just not having too many chances to succeed and being able to succeed in life is something that I cherish to the heart. So I give it my all because I take nothing for granted. And I just go out there and play the game hard. You never know when it's going to be the last time you put on that uniform so you might as well go hard while you're out there."

So how, if everyone knows he's going to steal when he enters a game, does he still manage to get away with it so frequently?

"Well, a lot has to do with counts," Dyson explained. "You look at pitcher's counts. What they like to throw in certain counts. Sometimes they're too quick for you to go. That's when you just have to pull the rabbit out of the hat right there. You got to dig back in your toolbox see what else is left that you can use, so you can see what kind of a read you can get on a guy. That's basically what I'm looking for. Just dig in your toolbox and I got a lot of things in my toolbox thanks to (Royals coach) Rusty Kuntz. He did a great job with us. Just having him around. He's been around the game for so long. He's helped each one of us with our game, whether it's base running, to defense, to bunting. It's just things; he's got so much information. And I take a lot of pride and joy being around that guy every day."

The Royals stunned the world in 2014 by making the playoffs for the first time in 29 years. This year, there were no surprises. They were the only team to reach postseason from the group that appeared in 2014 and they won their first World Series crown in 30 years. And Dyson was in the thick of things for both teams.

"Ah man, the goal this year from Day 1 of Spring Training was to win it all – and we did. Last year it was heartbreaking for us. We went on a magnificent run in the postseason and to get our heart broken in Game 7 at our home field sticks with you for a while. The whole offseason you just kept replaying that one play. You know, that pop up. They catch it. They celebrate on our home field. You know, I don't think I left this dugout for the first 15 minutes. Just looking at them. Watching them. Saying to myself, 'That's supposed to be us right there.' And I think that everybody went home, got their mind together, got their body, took care of their body and came back to spring with the same mindset. Like, 'Hey, let's try this again.' And since day one of spring, man, everybody's been ready. We're really ready to go. Seriously. The energy's been magnificent. Just everybody's on the same page and that's what you gotta have to win. You gotta have 25 guys on the same page, fighting for the same goal. And we did it. Man, we did it!"

And no professional team in Kansas City history has shared its success with the fans like the past two Royals American League and World Series championship squads.

"Gotta share it with the fans, you got to! Because it's been a long time since they've had some excitement out here and we just start winning, this organization just starts winning and it's been a long time. Like they said, 29 years. Last year we made a mark, made our mark and we took off. This year we brought it home, we finished it. We ain't just trying to get to the World Series to get there. We went to the World Series to win it. I want to finish first. Our team wants to finish first. We deserve it, our fans deserve it and our city deserves it."

CHAPTER 13

The Duffman

Danny Duffy was one of the most important components of the Kansas City Royals playoff machine in 2014 – starring in the second half of a season that now has been overshadowed by 2015's world title. But the likeable lefty, who now spends most of his time in the bullpen, has some fun recalling the craziest moments of 2014.

"We were fighting for our lives pretty much the whole month of September and we ended up squeaking into the Wild Card game," Duffy said. "We were lucky enough to get home field for that. It was quite a month. But it was, we learned a lot from it. It went by in a flash. But it was a lot of fun. We had never been to the playoffs before, the majority of us. So we were just trying to get there. It wasn't nerve-wracking or anything. We didn't know what was on the line. We didn't know that getting to Game 7 of the World Series was going to be something that would become a reality. We believed that we could do it, but we didn't know what was going to happen. We were just trying to get there. It was fun but it was quick. (It) happened really fast."

While Duffy won some of the biggest games of the second half of 2014, he found himself in the bullpen for the Wild Card game that many Royals fans thought would never be duplicated. Then, the 2015 Cardiac Kids won so many comeback games in the playoffs, it was nearly forgotten.

"It was fun being in the bullpen. It was fun. I was out there in the bullpen. I didn't partake in that game at all but I was exhausted afterwards, like I had been. A lot of drama. We never counted ourselves out. You could feel the emotion in the stands. The fans believed in us and you could just feel it. In the pen, we knew our boys were going to get it done. Just keep the line moving. I think we went 12 innings that day. And I was ready. It was me and Guthrie were the only two left in the bullpen to go. They got it done when they got it done. It was quite a day, quite a night.

"It was a different feeling watching from the bullpen. I'd never seen anything like it. I spent a lot of time looking up into the stands. People were extremely excited. It was a lot of fun to be a part of. I wish I could have been a little bit more of a part of it, but injuries held me back to 2 to 3 innings at a time, tops. But I'm thankful for everything that went down and just being able to be any kind of a part of it."

The biggest part of 2014 and 2015's success came from chemistry, a team concept in which the Royals are completely immersed. But Duffy believes the Royals mantra, if they had one, would be "fun."

"We have great chemistry, but it's also a lot of fun. I've said fun probably 14 times in these questions, but that's the best way I can put it. It's fun! It's great! I've been lucky enough to play with Hos (Eric Hosmer) and Moose (Mike Moustakas), Lorenzo (Cain). I've been pitching to Salvy (Perez) since we were 18. I like to think that I've come up with these dudes and helped us, in this process as much as I could. It's been great. It's been great. But chemistry is huge in this clubhouse. And anyone who says there's no such thing as clubhouse morale has never been a part of something like this. It helps us tremendously. We all treat this like a brotherhood. And when you are playing for more, there's something to be said about the focus that comes with it. It's huge. The fans know the history. I don't think there's a single person in this clubhouse who doesn't know what's happening right now. It's important. The fans deserve it. They've stuck with us since I was just a baby in this league. They deserve to be rewarded for it."

Duffy said there were many special moments in 2014, but one stands out from the rest.

"There were a whole bunch of them, but I would say the Wild Card game was No. 1. But clinching to go to the World Series was special I think, personally, for me. From a personal standpoint, getting into the ALDS in Game 1 and doing my part, as the entire bull pen did, in my home state against a team that a lot of people in my hometown root for...it was cool.

That was an amazing team that they had assembled, the Angels. We just fought and fought and fought. We were scrappy. And I respected them, but that was probably, personally, one of the most gratifying moments of my career. To just come in and get the job done, with what I had going on with my ribs. Just helping out. Just helping out. Being able to help was huge for me. Against a team of that stature. It was pretty special for me.

"And we believed in each other. The only people that matter – believing in us – is us. And our fans. The rest of the world could say whatever they want to say about us, but we believe in ourselves. And if we execute, we believe that we'll get the job done. There's nothing else to it. We don't need any projections or predictions on how our season is going to go. It's about the boys in here and getting it done ourselves and not worrying about what people say.

"I've known Hos since he was 18, I was 19. Me and Moose knew each other since high school. Pitched to Salvy since we were 18. Known Kelvin since he was 17. Known Ventura since he was 18. I could go on forever. Me and Tim Collins came up together. Let me look around. I mean, Greg Holland and I were in the same draft. I mean, I played with Scott Alexander in Idaho Falls in 2010. I've known Hoch since I was 18. Known Gordo since I was 18. I know all these dudes like the back of my hand. They are like family and there's something to be said for that. I could rattle off probably a couple more too, but you get the gist of it. Playing with these dudes growing up. Getting to know people on a personal level when you're growing, too. There's a lot to be said about that. There's not a bad dude in this clubhouse. We just pull for each other. We're like brothers on a Little League team. You're playing for a whole lot, but you're playing for each other more than you're playing for yourself and I think that's the biggest part of why we have done so well.

"We don't really feel any pressure. I guess the best way you could describe it is focus. The focus needs to be laser focus, needs to be in there 100%. We don't really feel any pressure. I think Rex Hudler said it best to me. He was like, 'Dude, when I was scuffling. I was hitting in the 100's. I took it upon myself to come into the clubhouse and just brighten everybody's day, no matter what. No matter how I was doing.' And I've had my fair share of struggles this year.

And I've had my fair share of days, probably four or five days, when I've come in and I was moody and somebody just picked me up. Somebody picked me up. And that's what we do. It's always addressed. It's always aided. Bad feelings, bad attitudes are always cured in here. On the spot."

Now that back-to-back American League championship seasons have come to an end, Duffy can enjoy himself this off season and spend some time sizing up his World Series championship ring. Or snuggling up in his bear suit that he wore during a postseason celebration that made him an internet sensation.

"That got a lot of attention," he said, grinning. "The guys wanted me to put it on, so I did. But I didn't expect to be interviewed on TV wearing it. But I did, and it was a lot of fun, for sure. Now that season is over, I'll have a lot of time for running. I love music – all kinds of music. I really like Revolution. It's a reggae rock group from Santa Barbara. I love reggae, Bob Marley obviously. I'm kinda' a Swiss Army knife with music, though. I've got something for everything, really."

CHAPTER 14

The Heart and 'J-Guts' of the Team

Jeremy Guthrie belongs to an elite fraternity as a member of the Kansas City Royals.

He is among a handful of pitchers who have won a World Series game, joining 2015 winners Chris Young, Johnny Cueto, Ryan Madson and Luke Hochevar, fellow 2014 winners Yordano Ventura and Kelvin Herrera, 1985 winners Bret Saberhagen (2), Dan Quisenberry and Danny Jackson, and Quisenberry and Dennis Leonard from the 1980 World Series squad.

He outdueled San Francisco's Tim Hudson in Game 3 of the 2014 Fall Classic, helping the Royals take a 2-1 lead at San Francisco. It brought back memories of a 12-year-old Guthrie watching Minnesota's Jack Morris pitch a 10-inning shutout in Game 7 of the World Series against the Atlanta Braves to give his team a world championship and 1-0 victory that will never be forgotten.

"I was Jack Morris for a little while," Guthrie said, grinning. "That was one of the special nights of my life – helping my team win a World Series game. I'd been in the big leagues 11 years and never been able to pitch in a World Series game and I wanted to make the most of it."

He certainly accomplished that. And while the Royals lost to the Giants in seven games, Guthrie made his mark both on and the mound and in the clubhouse of a team that had set in motion the wheels that would lead to a 2015 world title.

"Jeremy Guthrie – J-Guts – is my man," catcher Salvador Perez said, his voice soft and cracking with emotion. "I have never had a teammate like J-Guts, he is my brother. I love him. I want to work so hard behind the plate when he pitches because I want him to do well."

That statement caught the popular Guthrie off guard.

"He really said that?" asked Guthrie. "Really? That means a lot to me. I feel the same way about Salvy because he cares so much about everybody. I would never expect him to say those things. I would expect him to care that way about everyone but uh, to articulate it and say it you know, is very, wow. It's very humbling. So many things about being on this team are humbling. To do it like we did last year was amazing. No, no doubt about it. To accomplish what we did and then see everybody just mature so much and make the transformation from local stars to national superstars. (Mike) Moustakas, Lorenzo Cain, Eric Hosmer, Salvador, Yordano Ventura, the bullpen. To see these guys get recognition was really deserved.

Photo Courtesy Brad Penner-USA TODAY Sports

Nov 1, 2015; New York City, NY, USA; Kansas City Royals players celebrate with champagne in the clubhouse after defeating the New York Mets to win Game 5 of the World Series at Citi Field. The Royals won the World Series four games to one. In the middle of the fray, as he has been during his tenure as a Royal, is Jeremy Guthrie, sporting a snorkel as well as goggles. Many Royals point to Guthrie as one of the team's leaders.

"But now you come back the next year and it's not that anybody can do it once. That's certainly not the case. But to do it again and prove to everybody that this team plays the right way, this team plays hard, this team plays fundamentally sound, which allows us to compete in every baseball game is important. I think it's important that the guys in here, that the coaches show that to our fans. We weren't just a one-year wonder. But this is the kind of talent that a team can build on and go forever. So I think, I think everybody out here, I'd say went out sort of with a chip on their shoulder. They had a desire to prove to anybody that had any doubts about what we were able to accomplish last year was legitimate. I think that that was absolutely a focus for every one of these guys and still is."

Guthrie believes his team made great strides by winning the Wild Card game last year, but that the growth process was continuous.

"We can't grow up in one game, but it can certainly flip a switch of believing anything. I think for us it flipped the switch of 'this is house money.' We just escaped a game, that historically speaking, we had no, really no business winning against a pitcher who had thrown very well against us in Lester. You know to a situation that we were completely foreign to, every one of our players but maybe two or three that had that experience. When we got out of that one with a win, and flipped the switch on this city, to celebrate, now officially October baseball began. I think the result was a relaxed group of guys that then swept another very tough and very hot team in Anaheim. And then the possibilities were really endless after that. I was in the bullpen in that game and had a very surreal sense that it was very quiet in the bullpen. Everybody out there was all business. You know, focused on what they had to do. Which for me, it was pretty unfamiliar. I had not been in the bullpen all season. The moments, it was almost like the sounds of the game were delayed. You would see what was happening and you'd see the crowd stand up, but the cheers wouldn't get quite as deep to the bullpen for a few second. But that doesn't surprise me. That's the type of attitude we had last year. Enjoy what we're doing, play hard, have fun. And for our guys to re-focus on that in the seventh inning and then see what transpired afterward is a real credit to the guys. That there was nobody hanging their heads like you said. That there was no give up, but there was more a focus on enjoying it. And see what happens. And you saw what happened."

Raul Ibanez was a leader on the Royals team in the 2014 postseason even though he was not on the playoff roster. He would gather the younger players together and let them know what it took to win the big games. Guthrie took similar steps with the youngsters on the pitching staff.

"We have a bunch of guys on this team who are natural leaders. Some of them are younger in experience, some of them have been around a long time, but this team is full of guys that know how to lead, not only by example, but by their energy and their personality, so I, by no means, did I feel responsible in that regard. You know, just a piece that fit in the puzzle, that was the only goal. To hopefully be a part of something that was really really good. Last season was just so exhilarating. You know, one of those moments you certainly never forget as a player nor as a fan. I was warming up, so again, my experience was so different from the average teammate that was there cheering and hoping and preparing to run out on the field. My preparation was get my fastball down so when I get in there, I can get somebody out. Between pitches I'd stop and watch the pitch of the game and see Salvy (get the game-winning hit in the 12th inning). Immediately you drop the ball that's in your hand and run out to the field, so. It was, you know, it was more than you could have expected to have been a part, finally, of a playoff game, that knowing that the end of the day, one playoff game probably wouldn't have satisfied that appetite. Not as much as you wanted. And so it was very important to win and get in to a divisional series."

The Royals swept through the divisional series claiming every game as a victory. They did it with style and a confident approach that impressed their veteran teammate.

"I think there's always natural butterflies. Playing in an atmosphere and an experience they're not used to. It's going to cause a little bit of butterflies. But I believe that we play with a looseness that, having gotten into the playoffs, that was a big step for us. And having won that game in the Wild Card against all odds. There was a looseness and there was a calmness about how we were going to go to that series against the Angels. And, you know, you get a big moment in the extra innings with the Hosmer homerun and just another deep breath of fresh air, like you know, we can do this. We have a chance.

"To do it again...it just all kinda piled on top of each other. Play after play. Night after night. Big important moments. That different guys were stepping up and performing. And it was a different guy every night. Absolutely. It makes the team more unified. Different guys step up and are a part of important moments like that. Important team moments. Everyone felt like they were a vital piece of that puzzle in the playoffs. So it was, you know, I don't think you could have too many times where so many players are heroes on any given night. But we certainly had 'em."

CHAPTER 15

The Perfect Manager for this Team

Ned Yost has no idea why his team has its own barbershop, located near the lobby across from the Kauffman Stadium locker room.

He's not a fan of the choreographed handshakes and the only Salvador Perez dunk he truly enjoyed came on the infield at Citi Field after his Royals won the fifth and deciding game of the 2015 World Series. When jokingly asked if one day he might sport "The Hoz," the faux mohawk made so popular by first baseman Eric Hosmer, he said, "That's not going to happen."

Yet the winningest manager in Royals history lets his boys be boys. He wants them to play "fearlessly," and refuses to try and reign in a team that has as many individual personalities as it does talent. He is the perfect manager for the perfect team. He is also quite the story teller, and he used the World Series stage to tell a dandy.

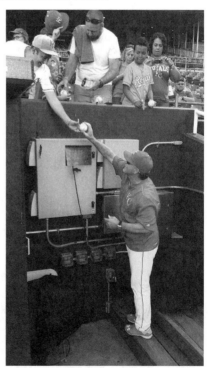

Royals manager Ned Yost takes a minute to sign an autograph for fans. Yost has led Kansas City to an unprecedented level of success.

"My uncle ran a bowling alley there in Jackson (Miss.)," said Yost, who was managing in the Mets AA farm system in the Mississippi community. "And they had a storage room out back. And that was my winter job. We'd go deer hunting and we'd do taxidermy in the back of the bowling alley back there. It was a lot of fun. The bowling alley is still there, but there's nothing in the back but old bowling balls and old pins."

That must seem like light years ago for a man who is at the height of his profession. He and Dayton Moore have created a team that redefined baseball. If his starting pitcher can make it through five or six innings with a lead, it likely means a victory as the Royals have the best and deepest bullpen in baseball. It was no accident that closer Wade Davis was on the mound in the 12th inning when the Royals closed out the Mets in a 7-2 Game 5 win.

"Wade got that last out," Yost said. "My heart was beating. You got Wade Davis on the mound, best reliever in baseball – you feel good. I have told these guys to play fearlessly, and they have responded."

Following the biggest win of his career, Yost discussed a wide variety of topics, including a surprise phone call from Washington, D.C.

"We made a great decision after we won Game 5. Originally, we were going to fly out after the game. But, with all the kids and family, we thought it could be a rough flight. If we win, everyone will feel better. If we lose, we'll feel better leaving the next day and have a good head of steam for

Royals manager Ned Yost (right) visits with members of the teams' scouting staff, including Royals Hall of Fame scout Art Stewart, to the left of Yost.

Game 6. So we win, and we leave the next day. While we're on the plane, I get a call. There is not Caller ID and that usually means a call from (Major League Baseball's chief baseball officer) Joe Torre. What does Joe Torre want? I answer the phone and someone asks, 'Is this Ned Yost. Can you hold and take a call from the President?' Sure. The next thing you know I am talking to President Obama. He said he is so excited for our organization, loves the way we play, and that we were a very exciting team to watch. We had a four or five minute conversation. It was pretty cool."

Almost as cool as the homecoming celebration that awaited the Royals as more than 800,000 fans poured into downtown Kansas City to celebrate just the second World Series championship in the history of the organization.

"The parade – our fans gave us the greatest gift they could give us and that is this turnout and a lifelong memory," Yost said. "I want to come back (and manage next year). I love being here and I feel like we are in a position where we can keep on winning. (But winning it all) is a weird feeling. I don't think it's sunk in yet. I thought I'd be jumping up and down and be so excited, but I feel like it's what we knew was going to happen and we went out and accomplished it. Hey. We won the World Series, it is very special, but deep in my heart it is something I thought we were going to do. I saw

Though it's probably fair to say his relationship with the media and fans has been a little rocky at times during his run as the manager of the Kansas City Royals, the affable Ned Yost is the toast of the town right now – after leading the Boys in Blue to back-to-back World Series and claiming the 2015 World Championship.

our players coming into spring training and I knew we were going to be right there – fun, exhausting – we set out to do it and we did."

After his team clinched their second postseason appearance in as many years, Yost sat down and talked about a season that would become maybe the most memorable in Royals history.

"We clinched it yeah, we knew what we needed to do anyway," he said. "And clinching was a foregone conclusion for us for a long time, so I think it was great for the city, it was great for our fans. We were able to do it at home. And be able to break a 30-year drought of winning a division. So that was special but we've got our eyes on a bigger prize. And thinking about that is really, really special. And these guys, from the moment they've gotten here, their focus was winning a championship and everybody loves to experience a championship. But these guys wanted to do it for our fans. And you would think that is lip service but notice every time we win. They come up they celebrate as a group up here for a little while then they all go back to the field to celebrate with our fans. They love it. And what Hoz and the boys did last year, I think it was down at the Power & Light District, they have a real connection with our fans. And it shows. In the ballgames, you can see the support. You know the fans feel a part of it. And these guys do a great job of including our fans in everything that we do.

"You look at Hoz, he's grown in leaps and bounds. He's very, very well respected in that locker room. He's a very level headed young man. He's tremendously talented, but I think what he does a lot of is lead with his mouth but he also leads by example. With the way that he goes about his business every single day. The way that he plays the game hard, every single day. He's just a special, he's a special person and he's a born leader. Everybody looks up to him. He doesn't get crazy. I think if you're going to lead, you have to have a steady personality. There are times to be serious. There are times to have fun. And he recognizes those times and uses it to his advantage. He's one of the most wonderful young men I've met in this game. And he's not the only leader. Alex Gordon leads by example – through his routines, through his work ethic, through his will to compete. Guys just admire that and when you see somebody that you admire, you naturally look up to them and follow his example.

"These are the guys who were playing well back in 2013 and that's when we really began thinking that 2014 and of course, this season, would be special. I felt like we'd really turned a corner. For me, and what my experience has been, this was my third go around from taking a team in dead last place and building it back up to a championship caliber team. I was a coach at Atlanta for 12 years and saw it happen. In Milwaukee we took a team that was fresh off a 106-game losing season and brought it back to the playoffs. And then we do it again here. My experience was when you get a group of players that come up together, as they did in Atlanta and Milwaukee and here. It generally takes them about two-and-a-half years before they can get themselves into contention. At that point, at the end of 2014, or 2013, that was about the mark. So you know I figured it would be a special year for us and it started out a little slow. I think we were six games under .500 at the All-Star Game break, then we really took off. You know, you just really knew that something special was going to happen."

A postseason that included a Major League Baseball record eight consecutive wins kicked off with a Wild Card Game for the ages – a 12-inning win over Oakland.

"Never seen anything like it," Yost readily admitted. "I don't think anybody has but the guys that played for Oakland and the guys that played for us. I mean it was an unbelievable game. You go through it and when it's over you are so worn out because of all the highs and the lows and you think, 'Okay, that was a good game.' And then we got to Anaheim the next day and every one of the Angels came up and they said, 'Man, that was the best game I've ever seen.' That's where it kinda' hits you, you know. It's like, 'Yeah, I guess that was a pretty good game.' It sure was a special experience. You know how, it's so funny, you get in such a zone. You don't really hear the noise. You feel it, but you don't hear it. And our guys were as focused as I've ever seem 'em. Especially in the eighth inning when they came in and we were down three runs, but they were doggedly determined they were not going to lose that game and you could hear them, 'We're not losing tonight! We're not losing to this pitcher! We're not losing to this team!' And sure enough, they went out, I think we were down four (7-3) and they ended up scoring three runs and tying it in the ninth and then, here we go. But it was just, the moment I think, when everything turned around was the eighth inning of the Wild Card game, when they came in that dugout and they finally believed who they were and what they could achieve. I don't know if they learned what it was like to win in that moment. It's just they finally believed in how good they were – we're unbeatable. You know we are a really, really good group and nobody can beat us and they went out and proved it."

Yost paused for a moment, before continuing.

"After that game was over they had confidence. They had everything they needed to be successful and there was no motivation needed. There was no nothing. They just had that look in their eye that you know, we're unbeatable. And we're going to go out and prove it. Oh, it's very special. It's tough going through it because every game was close. Every game was tight and there were a lot of extra inning games in there but everybody performed. When we needed a big hit, we got it. When we needed to get a big out, we got it. It was all kind of a blur, you know. You go into the playoffs. Really, the Wild Card game really wasn't the playoffs for me. If we lost the Wild Card game I felt like everything we'd accomplished the year before wouldn't have counted for anything, so once we won the Wild Card game, it felt to me like we were in the playoffs. And you know, yes, you're playing team with the best record in the California Angels and you know how tough they are. They've got Trout and they've got Pujols. They got great pitching. They've got a great manager. Great coaching staff. It's like, 'Okay, let's just go put on a good show. Let's go have a good series.' And to win Game 1 was like, 'Okay, Wow! That's great!' And to win Game 2, it's 'Okay, we've got this!' And the same thing with Baltimore. We went over there in their hometown and won the first two games and came back here and won Game 3 and it's like man, just unbelievable to win the American League Championship in four games."

And that set the stage for more drama and excitement as the Royals rewarded their fans with their first World Series appearance in 29 years.

"Going to the Series meant a lot," Yost said. "You saw what it did for the city and what it did for our fans. You know, it was a special time. The Kansas City Royals have always been a great organization. They've always had a phenomenal fan base. I remember playing against the Royals in the mid 80s, early 80s and how it was to come to Kansas City. And how the fans were just special. You just go to a place and hey, these guys are special. And we wanted to bring that back and we did. Again, the connection again with the fans and our ball team has been unbelievable. The TV ratings are up 90-percent. Attendance, we broke attendance records and it's just fun to be part of the Kansas City Royals now."

CHAPTER 16

The Architect

Dayton Moore has possessed the Midas Touch the past two seasons.

The architect of the best team in the American League planted the seeds when he arrived on the scene nine years ago, and now those seeds – with names like Eric Hosmer, Salvador Perez, Mike Moustakas, Greg Holland, and Yordano Ventura – are paying huge dividends. The draft picks, the trades, the behind-the-scenes wheeling and dealing have all resulted in solid gold results; the second world championship in the history of the team.

Moore spent several interview sessions last season talking about his team and his dreams. Those dreams coalesced into a reality in which the Kansas City Royals bested the New York Mets in the 2015 World Series – in five games no less – and saw them return home to a victory celebration downtown that drew an estimated 800,000 people.

No, that number is not a misprint.

"Let's talk about the parade," Moore said. "It was unbelievable. We got off the plane, got back from New York and someone said to expect 200,000 to 250,000 people. Well, I never heard the final total but I think it was around 750,000 and that doesn't surprise me at all. If you are in our community, you know how special our teams are. Kansas City has a great quality of life, and this city, our fans, are ready to support a team that brought so much respect to our community. It was a special moment and I hope we have several opportunities to do it again.

"That being said, I'm not sure it has sunk in yet that we are world champions. I snuck out to the dugout – as (Game5) unfolded – and I was in corner of our dugout during last out and I was able to share it with my family.

Baseball is the greatest game in the world – so many people can identify with it, it brings so much joy to people's lives. And to share that moment with my family, with Ned (Yost) and the players, was something I'll never forget."

Another moment he will never forget came while he was sitting on the side of Interstate-70 watching the Royals defeat the St. Louis Cardinals 11-0 in Game 7 of the 1985 World Series to claim their first world title.

"Well just by chance a buddy of mine by the name of David Larson," the personable general manager said. "We were both baseball players and students at Garden City Community College and we were coming back from Illinois, the Quad Cities. And coming through off I-70 on down to Garden City, and it just happened to be Game 7 of the World Series. Of course, it was a very special day for the Royals and baseball in general. A great series between the Royals and the Cardinals. So we stopped, tried to get tickets, realized that we probably couldn't afford them. So we noticed that there were several people congregating right off of I-70 and of course the ballpark was configured differently then. And we stopped and stood along the fence line up there. And you could see everything except left field. So it was fun. It was good. And the outcome was great. The Royals had a big blow out win and it was a great day for the Royals. I knew back then that I was going to be in baseball. I mean, that's the only thing I've ever thought about,

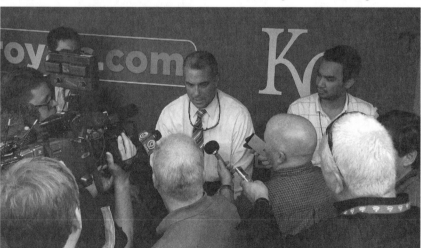

Kansas City Royals general manager Dayton Moore visits with the media in the Royals dugout. The organization has come a long way since Moore took over, but the rebuilding job he has completed has been nothing short of astonishing.

dreamt about, lived. I can never recall a day in my life, truthfully, when I haven't thought about this game. Never knew what a general manager did, of course. But at that time I wanted to play. I wanted to be able to play. And I was pursuing that aspect of it and finished up as a college player at George Mason University, signed with an independent pro team in the area, went to spring training with them, was released out of spring training and started my coaching career at George Mason University at that time.

"I was offered a couple of opportunities to scout and turned 'em down because I wanted to coach at that particular time. So I was coaching at George Mason and then managing in the Valley League in the summer and I was really enjoying my time. I was pursuing the college coaching career and then the Braves called and said they were interested in me becoming an area scout for them and I told them no. And then a guy named Roy Clark said, 'Just go down to Atlanta, meet with them, you've got nothing to lose.' So I decided to do it and I met with some special people and really enjoyed the conversation. I felt that if they want me to be an area scout, I was going to do it and I was going to try it for at least four years.

"One thing led to another and I had a chance to go down to Atlanta. I held different positions in the Braves organization. Learned a lot. Was around a lot of great people, a lot of wonderful mentors, and never really wanted to be a GM. It wasn't really a thing I pursued. And it just kind of happened."

Former Kansas City Royals general manager John Schuerholz became Moore's mentor and friend and, as they say in the movies, the rest is history.

"John's special. He's a great leader. A tremendous leader. Extremely smart. One of the most competitive people, if not the most competitive person I've ever been around in the game. He and Ned Yost are by far the two best competitors. John is a great competitor. He's a great competitor. And to have a guy like that have confidence in you, certainly makes you feel good. It motivates you to learn. It motivates you to do a great job. And of course it gave me a lot of opportunities so I'm forever grateful for John's support and his leadership."

It didn't take long before Moore began receiving phone calls about leaving his comfort zone with the Braves and becoming the architect for a championship team – like the Kansas City Royals.

"Well, probably about 2005 I began to get some calls. Teams asked permission to talk to me about those positions. Originally, I really wasn't interested because I loved the scouting and the development part of it. I loved working for John. I loved working for the Braves. I never really considered leaving. My family was thriving in the Atlanta area but you know when the Royals called, it was my boyhood team so we just pursued it a little bit, listened a little bit more, I guess. And even toward the end, I wasn't sure I was going to take the position, although it had been offered. And then we decided that you know what, let's go to Kansas City. Let's try to do something special and build a team, build an organization, help create a culture, and we've got a lot of wonderful people to support us. A lot of great people internally have done a terrific job leading and getting players and developing players. And of course our players have done a great job. And the fans have been extremely supportive and really helped create what is, now, an unbelievable environment and a great place to play.

"It took us a while, but we created a special culture in Kansas City. You have to, you have to create a great culture. And you have to create a place where people love to play, wanna work, and your leaders shape your culture. So you have to get good people in place and allow them to do their job, support them, and create an environment where people love to work. And our leaders do a great job of making sure that they're doing their part to make it a great place.

"We knew that we were going to create something special. I made sure I never set any deadlines or gave a year when we would accomplish our eventual goal. Our plan was simply to go to work every day and try to get better. Just do everything we can each day to try to get a little bit better. And try to get better each day. And then I would say repeatedly to our people, 'Let's try to get better each day and someday we'll wake up and we'll be pretty good.' But we knew in building the baseball team the way Mr. (David) Glass expected it, for us to do it, it was going to take eight to 10 years. We would take a kid out of high school, it's three, three and a half years in the minor leagues, if it goes really well. And that's another two to four years of playing each day at the major-league level to become a consistent producer. And we needed multiple players to do that. And we were going to have to get a little lucky. And I think we have. We've gotten some players that came on and have really done well for us. We've just tried to just focus on being as good as we can each day."

The Royals roster is now filled with the type of players Moore was talking about. Hosmer once said the highlight of his day was coming to the park and seeing his teammates. That comment brought a smile to the general manager's face.

"It's real important to have your players feel that way. These guys have grown up together, they've played together in the minor leagues, they've won together in the minor leagues. They have a genuine love and respect for one another. They pull for each other. They know each other's families. And they've had a lot of pride winning here in Kansas City. And they realized when we signed them that the Royals hadn't won in a long time. Not only not been in the playoffs, they'd not had a lot of winning seasons – and, just a couple really, over the course of many, many years. So they wanted to be the first group to do that, and they went to work every single day with an attitude that we're going to be the group to bring baseball back to Kansas City. We're very proud of them.

Moore seemed to have the Midas Touch in 2015, engineering signings and trades that all worked out remarkably well for the Royals. Kendrys Morales, Ben Zobrist, and Johnny Cueto were all brought on board, and all contributed significantly to a World Series crown.

"Taking a look back at 2014 – ending the postseason slump – we knew that we would make a run to be in the playoffs. It's hard to predict how you are going to do in the playoffs or if you will make the World Series, but we believed in this group because we know their heart was there, their heart was in the right place. They've got great passion to play and to give their best and they're just a terrific group of players. And so there's no doubt in my mind or any of our minds that we knew they had the right heart to play. And we knew we needed that one guy who had won, who could rally the young guys.

"Well trading young players is never easy. If you focus on what you're giving up, you'll make a deal to improve your team. But we knew we were going to start tilting the field in our favor. While our young players become the stars that we all dreamt that they would and envisioned that they would, we had to get good pitching. And we knew James Shields would bring a swagger and a toughness, a competitiveness that we needed. And, of course, Wade Davis has been equally as good and dominant and giving us that swagger as well. So, you have to do deals like that and as I said at the time, it's not, it's just the first of many deals that we're gonna have to do along these lines. You know, this past trade deadline, we had to move another good group of young, talented players in our minor leagues to support the efforts and the abilities of our current group here in Kansas City."

Again, Moore possessed the Midas Touch, as deals for Johnny Cueto and Ben Zobrist shored up an already strong team that was headed to uncharted territory. Those moves, combined with pre-season deals to bring in Kendrys Morales and Alex Rios, helped place the Royals on top of the baseball world.

"What this team has accomplished (the past two seasons) is very special. It's definitely an accomplishment for our fans, our community of course, and certainly the players and the entire organization. It's something that we felt was important from day one – to bring some energy back into our fan base. A fan base that has always been very supportive and passionate about this team, win or lose. And for us to be able to put a product on the field that they've embraced is a special feeling, and one we should all cherish and celebrate together."

As crazy as it might seem, there was a time in 2014 that Kauffman Stadium was not flooded by crazy fans who came early, stayed late, and rocked the rafters.

"We knew that people were following our team because of the television ratings, certainly the buzz around town if you will, and throughout our fan base. So we felt that with this group of players we're building, they will connect with the fans, and the way they play. It's an exciting team to watch. We all benefit from that. We all enjoy that. We all recognize that. I think that is something we all appreciate together, is the great energy and intensity with which these players attack the game. And it's special. And it's important to every fan base, but especially to the great people of the Midwest and the great people of Kansas City.

"They want to be able to identify with their players. That's why it's always been so crucial, so important to grow players from within. And be able to follow them from the draft. And through the minor leagues. To kind of live through their ups and downs. And pull for them. And celebrate their accomplishments. And then when they get to the major leagues. Our fans understand and they know when players are close to the major leagues. And when they break in and they have their debuts. They are excited to celebrate those monumental events in their careers. And our players want to give back to the fans, give back to the community.

"You know, I think they are tremendous people. They love playing the game and they've always understood, from Day 1, that it's important to connect with the fans. Our scouting people have understood that those are the types of players and people we want in Kansas City. Our programs in Latin America, we do the best we can to raise them to be the type of people that the fans in Kansas City want to embrace. And so certainly they get a lot of credit for signing the right types of players. Our development people do a tremendous job making sure our players are accountable. Once you have that type of culture and the players understand that, the players expect that of each other. They know it's how you should act as a professional."

While Moore will never spend a moment learning the intricate handshakes his players perform following big moments on the field, he can now accept their new brash style of baseball with a grin and a shrug of his shoulders.

"I've learned to like it I guess. At first, I'm kind of like, 'Just go do your job. Be a professional.' But you know, it's a different generation of players and Ned has done a great job of allowing these players to be themselves.

I think that he really deserves a lot of the credit for allowing some of the individualism, if you will. The way they respond. The raw emotion. He's kind of perpetuated that and allowed that to occur. I think it's important. I've learned to adjust, I guess.

"I think it's important. Let players play. Baseball's a fun game and you never want to take away the innocence of it. We all understand that and respect that. It's played by young men, but they still have the innocence of a little boy playing the game he loves."

Now, Moore stands center stage, holding the coveted World Series trophy he could only dream about when he came on board in 2006. This offseason brings new challenges, new dreams, and new territory. The hunters have become the hunted.

"I would hope that our success would help make the team even stronger in the offseason. But I've never been in this situation before. It's obviously a great joy winning the division, winning the A.L. championship, winning the World Series is great joy. It doesn't last forever, but it is a great joy. Our fans drive us and it's rewarding to share this with them. We will continue to work in a very intense way, we want to keep building and we're going to fight for our lives – that's what makes it fun and rewarding – like we did back in 2007, 2008 and 2009."

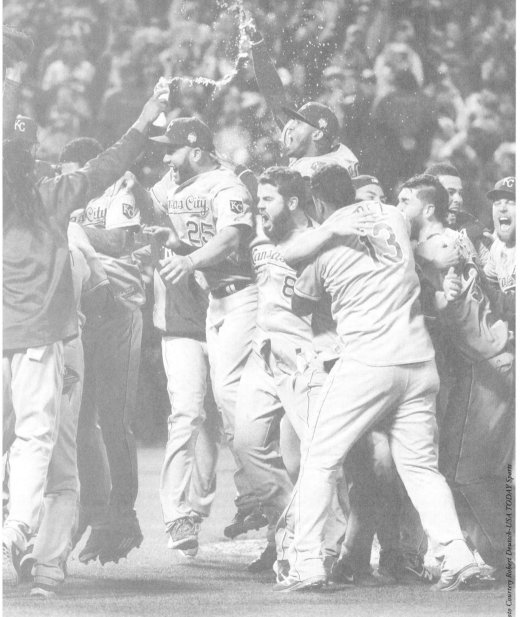

The Fans

CHAPTER 1

B. Royal

After her husband, Ben, was traded to the Kansas City Royals during the 2015 season, Julianna Zobrist would sometimes find herself walking through Kauffman Stadium when a complete stranger would stop to inquire about her health.

Now, at first blush, that probably seems a little strange. But then, not everyone is Julianna Zobrist; a successful Christian singer with a devoted following of her own and a bubbly, outgoing nature which spills over onto her television appearances and active use of social media.

Also, for the entirety of the Royals' remarkable run to the 2015 World Series crown, she happened to be glowingly – obviously – pregnant. So maybe Kansas City can be forgiven for seeming just as interested in she and Baby Z as in the outcome of that particular day's game.

"They'd say, 'We're keeping our fingers crossed for you,'" Julianna said. "And I'd say, 'I'm keeping my legs crossed, too. I don't want this little bundle of joy to arrive before the World

Photo Courtesy Julianna Zobrist

"Blaise Royal Zobrist waited for her daddy to win the World Series & came the day her mommy's single "Alive" dropped!"

Series is over.' It was all so humorous to me. We never thought we'd be in a World Series this year. Ben started the season with Oakland, then he comes over to the Royals and the magic starts to happen. I was amazed at how loving and caring the fans in Kansas City were to me and my family. Everywhere I went they'd come up to me with their fingers crossed, hoping our little girl waited until the series was over. And you know what? She did."

Blaise Royal Zobrist was born five days after her daddy's team won the World Series – claiming the title in 12 innings on a cool Sunday night at Citi Field in New York, with Julianna and their two children, 6-year-old Zion and 4-year-old Kruse, on hand.

That night marked the end of a personal and professional whirlwind for the Zobrist family. Traded to the Royals from the Athletics in late July, Ben immediately became a fan favorite in the City of Fountains due to his intelligent play, clutch hitting, versatility, and, well, his personality. He was a key cog in the Kansas City machine; a machine which relentlessly chugged its way to baseball's mountaintop.

"Oh, my goodness, the stories about the playoffs and the World Series – I have some good ones to tell," Julianna said. "There was all the talk about me going into labor and Ben not being with me. There was a good chance that would happen, but he was going to do everything possible to make sure it didn't. I was talking to him and he said, 'Babe, You may have to 'PJ,' it to New York,' I'm like, 'What? What do you mean 'P.J. it?' And he said, he was going to charter a private jet to take me, our kids and my doctor to the games in New York. I'm still like, 'P.J. it?' We're not 'P.J. it' people. We don't know any 'P.J. it' people, so I found that to be funny. But it shows what type of wonderful man I married. He hired a private jet to take me to the game, but we decided that I was not going to go to Citi Field unless the Royals could win the championship that night.

"So there I am, in my hotel room watching Game 3 on TV, and they lose. That means they can't win it the next night, so I stay in my hotel room the next night. Well, we all know they won that night, so I'm going to get to be with my family at Game 5 – and even though it took 12 innings, we won and we were the world champions of baseball. I think Zion and Kruse knew how big it was for their daddy, but I really knew how big it was. Ben might play a lot more baseball and never have the chance to win another World Series. It was such a special night and he made sure that his family was there to share it with him."

The Zobrists then returned to Kansas City and took part in the downtown parade and celebration that attracted more than 800,000 fans to downtown Kansas City.

"The parade was the one thing that really impressed our kids," Julianna said. "Zion is always around baseball, so it's no big deal to him. People ask him if he wants to be a player like his daddy and he just says, 'No,' and goes on his way. But before the parade started, you could tell he and Kruse were excited. We all rode in the back of trucks, and they wanted to know which truck was ours. When we finally got in our truck and started down the parade route, we were all so excited. None of us have ever seen that many people. I told the kids the people were there to see their daddy and his teammates and they thought that was pretty exciting."

The Friday after the Royals clinched the title, Blaise Royal Zobrist was born in Nashville.

Julianna posted on her Facebook account: "What do you name a little girl that so politely waited for the World Series to be won by her daddy? Then so sweetly thanked 800,000 fans at a parade, and the next day hung on while her family packed up and moved back home to Nashville? And then, in a brilliant finish, came to meet the world and say hello the day her mommy's new single 'Alive' is released? You call her a miracle. Or, we call her BLAISE ROYAL ZOBRIST."

Photo Courtesy Julianna Zobrist

The little diva didn't take a minute away from Daddy's contribution to the Royals

"OH MY WORD! OH MY WORD! OH MY WORD! OH MY WORD! Even though winning the World Series still feels like a dream, I have always known that he is a champion."

World Series championship with her entrance, but she did steal some of the thunder from the release of Mommy's single.

She didn't mind so much. Turns out, it's hard to be concerned with stuff like that when B. Royal Zobrist has captured your heart.

"A year ago, we had one thing circled on our calendar for that Friday," Julianna said, chuckling. "The release of my new single. Now, just think about it. Ben comes to Kansas City, we fall in love with the city and his new teammates, they go to the playoffs, win a World Series and Blaise Royal is born. We could feel the love from this city the minute we got here and we fell in love with Kansas City, but how on earth could you expect all those other things to happen? God provided so many wonderful things for our family, including Blaise's birth date."

When asked about her daughter's name, Julianna said, "We talked about the name Royal even before Ben came to Kansas City. It would be a strong name for a boy or a girl. Then, when he joined the Royals, it was the perfect name. And we didn't even think of B. Royal until someone mentioned it on Facebook. We were like, 'Yeah, that's great.' It just seemed right – perfect."

Julianna had jokingly posted to Twitter that if Blaise was born during a playoff game, she was going to tweet Ben a picture of his new daughter.

"I can only focus on one thing at a time anyway, she knows that," Ben said, of his wife, during the playoffs. "I'm one-track-minded. So it worked pretty well, I think, knowing that she can handle herself. And she's a strong woman,

Photo Courtesy Julianna Zobrist

so she's already kind of let me know that if we're in the middle of a game, she's probably not going to tell me anything that's going on. And that's fine, because I trust her and I trust the people that are around her, our family members that are with her and stuff right now. But she did tell me that I better hit a home run in a game if she

"You all are the craziest most beautiful fans!!! THANK YOU KANSAS CITY!!!!!"   is born while I'm playing and I'm not able to be with her at the hospital."

As it turns out, Ben did homer during the playoffs, but Blaise timed her arrival just right – making all the fuss a non-issue.

"It was all perfect, just perfect," Julianna said. "I tell Blaise every day what happened leading up to her birth. When she is totally milk drunk, just laying there, I tell her what happened and how an entire city was following her journey and how she made the playoffs and World Series so special for her new family."

And someday down the road, she's going to be able to ask questions and respond to her mother. Right now, these conversations are one sided, but that twinkle in her eye indicates that little B. Royal knows exactly what her mommy is talking about.

CHAPTER 2

Bleeding Royal Blue

I have been a Royals fan for as long as I could remember, mainly due to the fact I had older cousins who loved them in the late 1980s. They adored George Brett and since I viewed them as "cool," I followed their lead.

Little did I know how depressing most of my sports life would be.

Once Brett retired, my fandom included rooting for guys like Donnie Sadler, Desi Relaford, Mike Jacobs, Sal Fasano, Calvin Pickering, Roberto Hernandez and Chuck Knoblauch – many past their prime. Or, if we're being honest, never really had a prime in Major League Baseball. Years of losing starts to wear one down, as many Royals fans know. I never gave up despite hearing that Tony Pena will turn it around. Then, Buddy Bell will. Then, this manager from Japan, named Trey Hillman, is a diamond in the rough.

Nope. Nope. Nope.

My last few years living in Joplin (Mo.) I actually started to get hope in the future. With Northwest Arkansas and Springfield having Double-A teams close I was able to keep tabs on the up-and-coming players and the talent came in waves. I saw Kila Ka'aihue in the first wave, and then Mike Moustakas, Jarrod Dyson, Eric Hosmer, Salvador Perez, Danny Duffy, Mike Montgomery, and John Lamb all followed.

My first Royals playoff game came in 2010 in Springfield in the Texas League playoffs. Many of those same players were the reason I saw my first postseason game in Kansas City last year.

The World Series run was amazing as a fan. As a member of the media, I felt fortunate for the chance to be there and witness history. But, I'm a Royals fan first and foremost. The Wild Card game last year, in a way, gave me a chance to take in the game both ways.

I entered the game against Oakland with an uneasy feeling knowing the stakes. To me, the Royals weren't quite in the playoffs yet, so I didn't get my hopes up too much. I applied for credentials for my job – at the St. Joseph News-Press – and found out I had a seat in the second row of the press box. Tucked away in the far right-hand corner, I had to lean over to see home plate most of the time, but I didn't care. In all my years of reporting, I had never covered or even been at a baseball game with such lofty implications hanging on the outcome.

As many know, the Royals didn't start off well and when Yordano Ventura came into the game, it got worse in a hurry.

After the seventh inning, the Royals faced a 7-3 deficit so at that point, I made a decision. My day as a reporter would be over. Every since I moved to St. Joseph (Mo.) in 2010, I attended every single home finale and most times I worked my way down behind the dugout and cheered the team as they walked off the field at Kauffman for the final time each year. The first time I did that was vs. the White Sox in 2010 and I paid a whopping .67 for my ticket off StubHub. The 2013 home portion of the schedule ended with Justin Maxwell's walkoff grand slam; up to that point, one of the most intense games I've ever seen at the K.

My girlfriend, Samantha Asher, was at the Wild Card game as a fan and I told her I'd come down and watch the last few innings with her. I caught up with her in the right field concourse area at the bottom of the seventh. There were still a lot of people there despite the deficit so we found our way to the big TV and sat at one of the tables to watch the final few innings.

Sure it was just a coincidence, but the moment I gave up on a win, the team started to come back. In the eighth inning, the Royals trimmed the deficit down to 7-6. So I didn't move and stayed in that same spot in the ninth, when the Royals found a way to tie the game at 7-7. I was almost at a point of disbelief at what I was seeing. When Dyson scored the tying run, I was jumping around like a mad man out there – but luckily so were a number of other grown men – many like me that have only really known losing and Kansas City in the same sentence.

The game went into extra innings and we didn't move. Then, come the top of the 12th inning, the A's scored off the seemingly-invincible Brandon Finnegan.

For the second time in the night, the season was down to only three outs.

In hopes of fixing whatever mojo I thought we had that night, Sam and I moved around. Looking for another spot to watch the game, thinking that if we watch it on the same TV we lost the lead on, we'd lose for good.

We found a viewing spot in left field, next to the bar out there. I kept watching the game on TV because the last time I looked on the field, things weren't going well. Didn't want to jinx it. I saw the Hosmer triple on TV after I heard the crowd go wild. I saw Christian Colon's hit that scored Hosmer shortly after.

And in a moment I will never forget, I turned around and looked at the upper deck and all of the fans that stayed. While many left, there was still almost a sellout crowd cheering for a miracle and the 'Let's Go Royals!' chants raining down. With every pitch to Sal I felt the raw emotion of being a fan. I lived and died with every pitch knowing just one hit could end it. Also knowing one 'Sal swing' could send us into more extra innings.

Again, with my back to the field I watched the TV and then I heard the noise of the crowd. And then seconds later I saw the hit and Josh Donaldson's dive come up short.

I did what most fans did. I jumped up and down with joy. I screamed as loud as I could. Hell, I didn't really know how to celebrate a win like that because I had never even been in that position in my lifetime. My girlfriend told me that I picked her up at one point while jumping up and down. I have no recollection of that at all. I remember jumping up at one point and looking down and seeing her smile at my reaction. Maybe she was up in the air with me at that moment. I can't really recall that. But I realized how glad I was to be able to share that moment with someone I loved.

I knew before that night that I loved her but that night probably solidified me wanting to marry her.

Sam had spent two-plus years putting up with the roller coaster of emotions that I exude being a fan of the Royals. She tagged along with me to games many times, often not worrying about having to wake up early the next day. She had maybe one Royals t-shirt when we met and by the end of last postseason she was up to probably about 30. She began building the same love for the Royals and started to know the players – something I still get a giant kick out of even now.

I love Mizzou, the Chiefs, and the Missouri Mavericks, but nothing has compared to my love for the Royals when it comes to a team.

I use the word "we" every time I talk about them. I have a tattoo of the No. 5 on my ankle, because that is the number I wore in every sport growing up because I loved George Brett and wanted to be like him. I have a brick outside of Kauffman Stadium that I got the year of the All-Star Game came here.

That Wild Card game changed a lot in my life. The team took me on one of the wildest rides I have ever been a part of as a journalist, but more importantly, as a fan.

Like many men, showing emotions isn't a strong suit of mine, but as I got home that night of the Wild Card game I tried take in all that happened. I just kept playing back the night and couldn't believe it – I actually started to cry.

I spent my whole life pouring my heart and soul into rooting for this team and, finally, it paid off. Good things do come to those who wait. Like many, I endured the 100-loss seasons, I endured the ridicule for years of old co-workers and bosses who were Cardinals fan and believed it was a normal thing to be in the playoffs each year, and I endured liking a player – Damon, Dye, Appier, Saberhagen to name a few – and seeing him get traded away because that was just how things were in KC from 1990 to about 2009.

Dayton Moore built something I dreamed of happening. I led the Royals to tons of World Series titles on my Sega, Nintendo, or PlayStation over the years but for the first time in my lifetime it became plausible out here in the real world.

So to all of those who made it possible, thank you for creating memories I'll share with my grandchildren years down the road.

Cody Thorn
St. Joseph, Mo.

CHAPTER 3

The Homer That Almost Wasn't

Caleb Humphreys never dreamed he would become part of the drama when he attended Game 6 of the 2015 American League Championship Series between the Kansas City Royals and Toronto Blue Jays.

With one out, and the Royals leading 1-0 in the bottom of the second inning, the 2014 Blue Springs (Mo.) South High School graduate grabbed Mike Moustakas' home run that landed in the front row of the Pepsi Porch.

He was able to grab the prized home run ball in front of his brother Haden, a South freshman, as the Royals went on to win 4-3.

"We never sit anywhere where we have the chance to catch a fly ball, so we brought our gloves," said Humphreys, a standout pitcher on the South baseball team that finished third in the state in 2014.

A graduate of Blue Springs (Mo.) South High School, Caleb Humphreys caused a brief controversy during Game 6 of the 2015 ALCS at Kauffman Stadium. The young man snagged a home run hit by Mike Moustakas, which was reviewed by Major League Baseball officials in New York City, to determine if Humphreys had interfered. After careful deliberation, they decided he had not, and the home run stood.

"I never dreamed I'd have the chance to catch a home run ball, especially a home run ball from Mike Moustakas."

That dream suddenly turned into a nightmare as Toronto manager John Gibbons asked for an umpire's challenge, to see if Humphreys had interfered with a ball in play.

"The first thing I thought was, 'Oh no, they're going to call it an out! Where am I going to hide?'" Humphreys said. "Then they ruled it a home run, and I never felt so good. I'd have hated to have been thought of like that guy in Chicago (Steve Bartman) who interfered with the outfielder and everyone said he cost the Cubs a chance to win that playoff game."

Humphreys became an instant celebrity as fans asked to have their photo taken with him, along with the home run baseball.

He was even interviewed by Fox Sports' Erin Andrews.

"I didn't even know who she was," Humphreys admitted.

Humphreys is now attending Metropolitan Community College-Blue River and said, "My playing career is over, but I like being able to come to a Royals playoff game and catch a home run ball. This is pretty cool."

Humphreys hopes to meet Moustakas and have him sign the ultimate playoff souvenir.

"The only thing better than catching the homer would be to meet Mike and have him sign the ball," Humphreys said.

CHAPTER 4

Antler Man

Craig Rookstool is everywhere – posing for photos with excited Kansas City Royals fans, starring in a national Major League Baseball postseason commercial, and visiting with members of his favorite baseball team.

So, who is Craig Rookstool? You might be more familiar with his nickname, "Antler Man."

Before Game 1 of the 2014 World Series, Rookstool, the CEO and owner of Lee's Summit (Mo.)-based AvidAir International, made a spur-of-the-moment decision to order a pair of $300 replica/life-sized moose antlers from Cabela's.

Die-hard Royals fan Craig Rookstool purchased a $300 set of replica moose antlers from Cabela's, as a gesture of support for Royals third baseman Mike Moustakas, and quickly became a fixture on the jumbotron at Kauffman Stadium.

"I guess you could say the rest is history," said Rookstool, who graciously took a few minutes to visit about his new-found celebrity status at the Kansas City Royals Postseason Celebration at Kauffman Stadium. "I was sitting around home, trying to think of a way I could honor Mike Moustakas (the Royals all-star third baseman) and I got the idea of buying some antlers.

"At the time, I didn't even know if they would let me bring them into the stadium."

They did – and he became as big as a hit as the Moustakas-led Royals that made the postseason in 2014 for the first time in 29 years.

"It was kind of crazy," Rookstool said. "I was bringing them into that first World Series game, and there was security everywhere," he explained, as he took a rest from holding the 10-pound antlers above his head, or the head of any fan that made a special request. "I looked at the security people, and they were all smiling and laughing near Gate E and waving me on through. That's my gate, and it was easy to get in."

Getting to his seat was a different matter.

"When I was walking down to my seat (a few rows behind the Royals dugout), I found out that (former Kansas senator and presidential candidate) Bob Dole and a three-star general were sitting in my section," Rookstool said, chuckling. "Their security wasn't too happy with this guy coming down with antlers on his head. I didn't know what was going to happen, when a security guy I knew came down and said, 'MLB just showed you and had 50,000 hits on its website.' I knew after that there was no way they were going to make me leave and take my antlers with me."

The longtime season ticket holder, who attended the 1985 World Series, is now a mainstay at the stadium.

"He's the best," said one fan who waited in line several minutes to have her photo taken with Rookstool. "It's tough to come out and meet a player or get an autograph, but we know we can get our picture taken with Antler Man."

Young, old, new fans or old fans, they all love Rookstool – and he's getting more and more accustomed to the attention.

"I didn't do this to get on a national commercial – that was the furthest thing from my mind," said Rookstool, who attended spring training in Surprise, Ariz., this past February and was able to meet Moustakas and many of his teammates – who were more than happy to autograph the antlers. "I just wanted to do something fun to honor Mike and the fact that the Royals were back in the World Series for the first time in 29 years."

The players love Antler Man as much as the fans.

"It's great," Moustakas said. "The first time I saw the guy I thought, 'Man, that guy brought antlers to the stadium? Cool.'"

Now, Rookstool is spreading awareness for his favorite non-profit organization, Peace Partnership (www.peacecounseling.org). The Lee's Summit-based counseling center helps provide education and works with financially disadvantaged families. It is totally funded by donations.

"It started off as fun, but now, let's bless some lives with this," Rookstool said. "With the help of Royals Charities, I am going to auction off these antlers and all the money is going to Peace Partnership."

CHAPTER 5

"KCMO Anthem"

When Gold Glove first baseman Eric Hosmer strides to the plate at Kauffman Stadium, he is accompanied by his walk up song, "Hood Go Crazy," by Kansas City icon Tech N9ne.

Tech is one of the biggest Royals fans on the planet. You could see him sitting in the front row right behind home plate at each of the first two World Series games, and a demanding tour schedule took him away from his Boys in Blue after they left for New York. But he found a way to reward them for their second world championship by honoring them with his latest song, "KCMO Anthem."

He laid down tracks at his Strange Music studio in Lee's Summit less than 48 hours after Wade Davis recorded the last out in Game 5 versus the New York Mets, putting an end to the 2015 World Series.

"I was so happy – so very happy – my boys in blue won the World Series," Tech said. "When they won it, the song just came out of me like water, it just poured out of me. I had just done my

Hip-hop icon and Kansas City native Tech N9NE was so excited by the Royals' World Series victory he quickly took to the studio and composed their own song – which he dubbed the "KCMO Anthem."

Halloween concert in Maine, and the pilot was giving updates of the score. It's like Mets 2-0 and we're going from Maine to Baltimore for a layover. We get back on the plane and head to Kansas City and it's like 2-2. 2-2?!? What! That's fantastic. When we tied it up in the ninth, I just knew we were going to win. When we landed, everyone in the airport was watching the TV's. There were hundreds of people crowded around every TV, including me – and when we won, I just put my head in my hands and said, "My God, we did it. We're world champions.' So I called up Seven, my producer and we headed for the studio. We got there about 7:30 the next day and had it done by 9 or so. And I'm so happy with it. It's my 'KCMO Anthem,' to the town I love and the team I love. I love going out to the stadium, catching the game, talking with the players. I'm like a little kid. Now, I get to honor them with their own anthem."

While Tech had the best seats in the house at the Royals' two World Series home games, he also scored the best seat for the downtown celebration that attracted more than 800,000 people to the area around Union Station.

"I was on the 15th floor of the Westin Crown Center and got to see everything," he said. "Man, it was beautiful. But there was one problem – you couldn't find any food anywhere. You call for a pizza and they said, 'Two hours.'"

So Tech and his friends went throughout Crown Center and ran into a security guard who recognized the man Rolling Stone calls "Rap's Indie Trailblazer."

"This guard was great, and he took us into one of the ballrooms, where there was supposed to be an event and they cancelled it because of the parade and the celebration. But they didn't cancel the food. Man, they had turkey, lettuce, tomatoes, cheese, croissants, soda – you name it – so we grabbed it all up and took it back up to our room on the 15th floor."

But they were soon stopped by another security officer who was unaware of what had happened with the cancellation.

"I finally found the card of the guard who let us take the food, showed it to this guy, and as it turned out the guy who let us have the food was this guy's boss – so it all worked out great," Tech said, chuckling. "We were eating good, watching the parade, the celebration at Union Station."

CHAPTER 6

"We're not heroes..."

During a memorable postseason run, the Kansas City Royals paid tribute to two fallen heroes, longtime Kansas City firefighters Larry Leggio, 43, a Fire Apparatus Operator with 17 years experience, and John Mesh, 39, of Pumper 10. Both were killed Oct. 12, 2015, when a portion of a wall collapsed inside a burning building in Kansas City's old Northeast neighborhood. Leggio and Mesh were working with their colleagues to rescue two individuals caught inside, who were safely retrieved.

Eric Hosmer and many of his teammates wore shirts and caps emblazoned with the KCFD logo, and the Gold Glove first baseman – whose father was a 29-year veteran of the fire department in Liberty City, Fla. – spoke about the tragedy and the impact it had on his team and his city.

"On behalf of the Kansas City Royals and myself included, we just want to let everybody know that our thoughts and prayers are with the Kansas City Fire Department," Hosmer said, softly. "Obviously it's very crazy what happened, and for me, personally, it hits

Royals first baseman Eric Hosmer, whose father is a retired fireman in Florida, showed his support of the Kansas City Fire Department the day after a downtown blaze claimed the lives of two local firemen in October.

really close to home, having a father being a firefighter for 29 years. And I just remember plenty of times on the phone with him and him having to hang up and go on a run. And as a family, it's always a tough time and you're always a little nervous to wait for a call back from him and see what's going on. So, I was fortunate to never have a phone call from the fire department saying something crazy happened, so I can only imagine what the families are all going through.

"But that's a special thing about Kansas City and this team, this city. The bond that we have with our fans and in our community is really something I've never experienced before, being from a big city like Miami. And we just want to just extend our prayers to the family and let everybody know that obviously there's nothing we can do to make this go away or make this disappear, but as a team, as a city we're all going to unite and just try and get through these times with each other. And, like I said, we just want to extend our prayers to them and on behalf of myself and everybody in that locker room."

Hosmer found out about the accident, like many of his teammates, while scrolling through social media before heading to the ballpark.

"I first heard about it this morning, actually, just kind of on my phone, looking through Twitter and reading the whole entire story and stuff. So, I've met a couple of the firefighters that work here throughout the stadium, and as my dad came and visited he's gotten to know a lot of the guys as well. So it's a tough time, but we're all in it together. And this is was what makes Kansas City such a special place, is everyone rallies up for times like this and really just leans on each other for support.

"It's something that it hits really close to home for me personally. It's terrible to wake up and see the news, especially around this time of year with a lot of exciting stuff going on in Kansas City. But that was the reason we all wore the shirts today and we all wore our hats, was just to let everybody know we're behind them 100-percent and we're going to try and get through this as a city, as community, all together."

While growing up, Hosmer said his parents did a great job keeping him isolated from the dangers his father faced every day on the job.

"Well, that's one thing my parents really did well with my brother and me, was we never realized how dangerous the job actually was until becoming a little older and actually knowing what a firefighter does and what the job consists of. It's nerve-wracking, because my dad would work 48-hour shifts and would be off for 24 hours. And like I said, whenever you're talking to him on the phone and you can hear the bell ringing from the station, that he's got to go and he has a run, and there's always a little just slight nerves that something crazy can happen.

"And fortunately enough for me and my family nothing like that he's ever happened. So I just can only imagine what they're going through. I know being in the locker rooms and at the station, at the firehouse, these guys have similar relationships to what we do in the locker room in there, so I know they're going through tough times right now. And, like I said, we just want them to know that we have their backs 100-percent."

Had baseball not worked out for the newest world champion Royal, he would have followed in his father's footsteps.

"For me personally, if I didn't become a baseball player, that was the career I was going to pursue. I grew up in a firehouse. My dad worked about 30 minutes from where we lived back home, and my grandparents lived close to where my dad's work area was, so any time we were in the area we would always stop by the station, always go and visit the guys. And just seeing the bond that they have, there's a lot of similarities to the bond we all have in the locker room here. And just seeing my dad interact with some of the firefighters around here, and it's the same terms that they all use, everyone, they say hello to each other, and before they leave everyone says 'stay safe.' And it's the common term that the firefighters all get, it's obviously a huge fraternity that – it's something I remember when the Marlins were battling the Cubs in 2003 I believe in the playoffs, my dad telling me how the city of Miami had a fun bet going on with Chicago's fire department and whoever won the series would send them shirts. So you know how close the firefighter community around the world is, so just something that me growing up in a firehouse just wanted to reach out and let them know we're behind them."

While Hosmer and the Royals are Kansas City's heroes – as evidenced by the more than 800,000 fans who jammed downtown streets during a memorable celebration – Hosmer said he is not a hero.

"You look at guys throwing a game-winning touchdown or hitting a game-winning home run, and we all want to classify them as heroes," Hosmer said, "But we're not heroes – firefighters are the real heroes. And to some extent, obviously, it's fun to watch sports and how they interact like that, but when you're talking about real-life situations and houses burning down and people willing to sacrifice their lives and put their lives behind somebody else to go in and save them, it just truly defines what true character is.

"And any time – for me personally – any time you put your life at risk to try and save somebody else's, that just alone I think explains the type of person that you have to be to be a firefighter."

CHAPTER 7

How a Haircut Took Over a City

It's called "The Hoz," and it is possibly the most talked about hairstyle since Farrah Fawcett hooked up with Charlie and some Angels back in the 1970s.

But it doesn't belong to a Hollywood bombshell. No, The Hoz sits atop the head of Eric Hosmer, whose late-game heroics played a huge role in the Kansas City Royals claiming the second World Series championship in the history of the franchise.

There are many positives, call them perks, that come with being a Major League baseball player. One of those perks, if you're a Royal, is the presence of a barber shop – yes, a full-service barber shop – in the clubhouse, to keep the players looking fresh at all times.

It was in this barber shop, which sits complete with an old-school barber pole outside the door, that The Hoz was born. And from that barber's chair, it spread to the heads of children, and more than a few grown

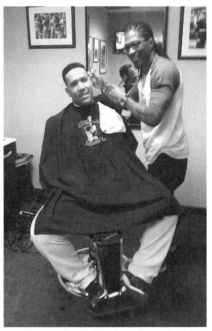

DeJuan Bonds is the barber Royals players go to when they want to look sharp for game day. Here, Bonds, who has his own shop adjacent to the Royals locker room, puts the finishing touches on the always-stylish Salvador Perez.

men, throughout the Royals fanbase. Today, it's maybe easier to identify an Eric Hosmer fan by his haircut than by the No. 35 jersey on his back.

Who better to describe the story behind a bona-fide Kansas City cultural phenomenon than the man who created it?

DeJuan Bonds is a barber by trade; one who spends his days at the Purple Label Deluxe Barbershop in Overland Park, Kan., and his evenings at Kauffman Stadium tending to the follicular needs of the players and coaches.

"It all started out as a regular mohawk," Bonds said. "But every player wants something different, something unique, so we tightened up the mohawk, made a few modifications and I listened to a few suggestions from Hoz, and before you know it, 'The Hoz' was born."

Bonds didn't realize what a big deal his cut had become until he had

Perhaps the only thing that gets Eric Hosmer more attention than his Gold Glove fielding and timely hitting is his hairstyle, which has been popularly dubbed, "The Hoz."

a conversation with a patron in a metro area sports bar.

"I was sitting at the bar, and a young lady came and sat down next to me," Bonds said. "We got to talking about baseball and I asked her if she liked the sport."

As it turned out, she wasn't going to be naming the starting lineups of the 1985 Royals, but she liked the sport well enough. Though she really took an interest in No. 35 and his "cool hair."

"I heard that and couldn't help but grin," Bonds said. "We got to talking some more and I told her I was a barber, and she asked, 'Have you done many 'Hozes?'"

Bonds couldn't help but smile.

"I just about cracked up," he said. "I told her I'd done a few. Well, she keeps talking about Hoz's hair and I had to tell her that I was the one who came up with it. She went kind of crazy and wanted to take a selfie.

But Bonds is old-school, and a hastily-snapped close-up wasn't going to do.

"I told her I wasn't into selfies," he said. "But we got someone to take a nice picture, and I think she was pretty happy."

When that story was relayed to Hosmer, the Gold Glove first baseman could only grin.

"Really, yeah, DeJuan's the man," Hosmer said. "We tell him, 'If we look sharp, we play sharp.' He takes care of us. We can walk right across the lobby and get our hair cut. It's pretty sweet. We have some good conversations. He's a good man, we love DeJuan."

And not just for his mastery with the shears or his ability to listen. Ever the superstitious lot, baseball players will look for any possible edge to break a slump or produce a big game. A new pair of socks? Sure. Some new shoes, or a new type of food for lunch? Why not?

A new haircut? Absolutely.

"They walk in and say, 'Put a hit on me!'" Bonds said, chuckling. "They like to look good and I want them looking good. I want them getting those hits – and if they think I had something to do with it, great!"

Bonds has become a friend, confidante, father figure and friend to Royals players like Hosmer, Jarrod Dyson, Omar Infante, Paulo Orlando, Alex Rios and Salvador Perez.

Kendrys Morales, who speaks little English, is a frequent visitor to Bonds' barber digs.

"Man, I have to learn Spanish," he said, a little ruefully. "I'm thinking about getting those CDs so I can listen and learn in my car. I'd like to converse with Kendrys. He is such a great guy, but we don't really talk that much. When I'm finished with him, he just looks in the mirror and says, 'Oh, baby.'

"I like that."

CHAPTER 8

This Town Bleeds Blue

What follows is a collection of vignettes from the 2014 and 2015 seasons, each offering the perspective of someone different who all share one thing in common – a love of the Kansas City Royals

Shortly after the Kauffman Stadium gates opened at 10:15 a.m., the morning after the 2014 Major League Baseball season came to a close, the lower bowl of the stadium was packed with a crowd that filled the seats from behind the Royals dugout down to the left-field bullpen.

They carried signs and wanted their Royals to know that even though they lost Game 7 of the World Series 3-2 to the San Francisco Giants just hours before this season-ending pep rally, the Royals had re-established pride and developed a bond with a fan base that everyone in the nation was talking about.

"Be loud and be proud!" Kansas City Mayor Sly James said as the fans hooted and hollered and showered him with affection.

"Kansas City baseball did not just become relevant when we started winning and appeared in the postseason – this team has been relevant all my life!

"I have followed them every day – win, lose or draw – and I am proud of them and I am proud of you, Kansas City. Because of you, baseball fans all over the world are talking about our team, a team that mirrors all of you, for its enthusiasm and desire. Today, we are all Royal!"

As the fans continued to stand and cheer, he added, "Don't look at last night as a loss. Look at it as the beginning of dynasty!"

County Executive Mike Sanders attended the rally with his sons and gave the fans plenty to cheer about.

"I have never been more proud to be a Royals fan than I am today," Sanders said. "We need to relish this team, honor this team and hope for more Blue Octobers."

One by one, members of the Royals front office came out of the team dugout, and their reaction to the massive crowd was one of awe and delight.

""It is truly an honor to have this many of you come out and honor our team today," said general manager Dayton Moore. "Losing is not fun. It hurts today, but I can tell you that our motivation to keep going forward is as strong as it has ever been.

"I am so proud to be a part of Kansas City and I want to thank all of you for coming today."

Team owner David Glass was the last Royals representative to speak before MC and Royals announcer Ryan Lefebvre turned the mic over to manager Ned Yost and the players. As Glass walked up the steps to the field the fans clapped and cheered "Let's go Royals!" which brought a smile to the owner's face.

"To have all of you here is so special," Glass said. "We wanted the opportunity to thank you for all your support. Without you, none of this is possible."

That heightened the cheering and applause.

"And we need to thank Dayton, Ned, the coaches and the players."

The roar was deafening as Yost led out 11 players and coaches who made one final trip to The K in 2014 and the ovation could be heard throughout Eastern Jackson County. As he waited for a teammate to take the field, catcher Salvador Perez looked at the crowd and said, "Amazing, this is just amazing."

Despite the fact that Perez made the final out of the heartbreaking loss to the San Francisco Giants, the All-Star catcher wanted to say goodbye to the fans who made the postseason run so special.

"They were with us every game," he added, "and we need to thank them."

He then spied a "MARRY ME PEREZ" sign and chuckled.

There were a lot of smiles, thanks, and even an occasional laugh as manger Ned Yost and his team took one final bow while most memorable season in 29 years came to an end.

"After last night, I don't think any of us wanted to get out of bed today," Yost said, as his players nodded in agreement. "But the reason we got out of bed was to thank you! You had our backs the entire postseason. We loved it and we appreciated it!"

After that comment, the manager who is often a lightning rod for fan controversy, received the biggest cheer of the day.

The microphone was then turned over to the man credited with changing the mindset of an entire team, starting pitcher "Big Game" James Shields, who taught a young, untested team how to win.

"Everything we did on the field, we did for you," Shields said. "You were part of everything we accomplished. Every little kid dreams of playing in a World Series, and we got to experience that. And we were able to share it with you."

Designated hitter Billy Butler had been a part of the Royals since he was 18, and signed with the Oakland Athletics following the 2014 season.

He battled his emotions as he thanked the fans, who oftentimes drowned out his comments with their cheers.

"Thank you for treating us like royalty," he said, his voice cracking.

As American League Championship Series MVP Lorenzo Cain took the microphone, a voice from the stands cried out, "We love you, Lo!"

He smiled and said, "Love you guys, too. Thanks for all the support."

After rookie Yordano Ventura did an impromptu dance and Kansas City Mayor Sly James presented each of the members of the team and coaching staff a Royal blue bow tie, the players disappeared back into the dugout with the clapping and cheering ringing in their ears.

• • •

Memories.

We all have them.

For some, the memories of the Kansas City Royals' 1985 World Series triumph are so vivid and colorful it's like they happened yesterday.

That's certainly the case for longtime Eastern Jackson County resident and Royals fan Cathy Stacker, who attended the 1985 Fall Classic and kept a spot-on scrapbook to keep all those memories alive.

"It's kind of funny how I became a fan," said Stacker, 70, who is following each and every minute of this year's Royals World Series team. "We lived close to the stadium when it was being built, and I guess because of all the construction and the noise in the area, the Royals sent out tickets to people who lived in the neighborhood.

"This beautiful stadium was being built, I had free tickets, so I started going to the games. And I was hooked, I became a big fan."

And soon, some of the players and umpires became a fan of her work, as she designed decorative bands for Cowboy hats.

"I don't know if you remember the Englewood Opry, but Johnny Lee and Mickey Gilley came there to perform and they saw the hatbands I had made and wanted me to make them some," she explained.

Beloved Kansas City Royals mascot Sluggerrr the Lion has worn a crown for years as King of the Jungle, and now his team has brought home one as well in 2015.

"Then, an American League umpire saw my hatbands and we became friends and he helped me get tickets to the 1985 World Series. I even made a hatband for George Brett, but I'm sure he doesn't even remember it."

Her tickets were just $30 per game, and she took care of her family and friends and attended each contest at then-Royals Stadium.

"I have so many wonderful memories and I am so thankful I kept a scrapbook," she said. "I can look at it, and remember most of the plays from every game. I remember Bret Saberhagen pitching and George Brett playing so well. Oh, I just remember all of it."

Her scrapbook includes photos of her in a fancy cowboy hat, complete with an eye-opening hatband, ticket stubs, bumper stickers and photos of the celebration following the big win in Game 7 over I-70 rival St. Louis.

"My sister lived close to Larry Gura, and he even gave her a baseball signed by the team," she said, with a touch of pride in her voice.

"And now, we're 8-0 (in the playoffs, at the time of the interview) and going back to the World Series. I just love this young team. They all seem so nice, especially Salvador Perez – he is always smiling – and they are sharing it with us. And that makes it even more special."

• • •

Logan and Paige Tucker weren't too thrilled with their mom, Heather, before Wednesday night's Kansas City Royals game.

She was running late from work, still had to print off the tickets for that night's game and the children wanted to get there early to catch some of the pregame festivities.

Little did the Tucker family realize they would be a big part of those festivities, as they were named the recording-breaking 2,477,701st fans to enter the stadium, snapping the team's the single-season attendance mark.

Tony Tucker of Blue Springs, Mo., walked through Gate E a little after 6 p.m., with wife Heather and their two children and they were greeted by Sluggerrr and members of the K-Crew. They received a framed certificate, ticket upgrades to front row seats in the Crown Club and a jersey signed by the 2015 team.

"We really had this down to a science," said Toby Cook, the Royals vice president of community affairs and publicity. "We had real time monitoring at all the gates and we settled on selecting a fan from Gate E (the main gate located at the southeast side of the stadium). We had four seats in the Crown Club, so we were looking for a family of four and the Tuckers were perfect – mom and dad and a son and daughter."

Heather knew something was going on, but she was not sure what to make of it.

"This guy was following us, and I'm wondering why," the protective mom said, grinning. "Logan stopped to tie his shoe, and this guy stopped and I really began to wonder. Then, I saw Sluggerrr, Toby Cook – who I recognized from seeing on TV – and the K-Crew. Sluggger came with a

Sal Perez water container and I'm thinking, 'Please don't get us wet,' and he didn't. It was full of glitter."

The family was then told they were the record breakers and their night of a lifetime began.

"I can't wait to get to school tomorrow," Paige, 13, an eighth grader at Moreland Ridge Middle School, said Wednesday. "I'm going to be the most popular kid in school for one day. I can't wait to tell everyone what happened."

Ditto for Logan, 9, a fourth grader at Cordill-Mason Elementary School.

"It's the coolest thing that ever happened to me," said Logan, who saw Hall of Famer George Brett in the Diamond Club and also got him to sign the special jersey. "A ball was hit up (in the Diamond Club) and I went after it, but a man got it. Then, he handed it to me. This is the best night ever."

• • •

As he watched the Kansas City Royals post-2014 American League Championship champagne party in the champagne soaked locker room, a touch of nostalgia washed over Missouri Mavericks coach Richard Matvichuk.

"I was watching on TV here in the office with Brent (Thiessen, president and general manager), Watty (Simon Watson, assistant coach), Bill (Murray, trainer, who was part of the New Jersey Devils' Stanley Cup wins in 2000 and 2003), Drew (Andrew Dvorak, equipment manager) and Clint (Elberts, goaltender coach) and I remembered how satisfying it was to work so hard, and get a reward like a championship."

While the Royals were celebrating an ALCS championship and their first trip to the World Series since winning their lone championship back in 1985, Matvichuk and his Dallas Stars teammates won the Stanley Cup in 1999.

"I watch those kids on the Royals and you can just see how much they care for each other," the coach continued. "You can see the satisfaction on their faces – they're so close – and that's what it takes to win a championship.

"Well, that and great pitching and defense."

Both of which have been the two hallmarks of the Royals remarkable 8-0 postseason run. They are the first team in Major League Baseball history to go 8-0 in the playoffs. The 1976 Cincinnati Reds and the 2007 Colorado Rockies each went 7-0.

"I'm glad they don't have to wait long for the Series to start," Matvichuk said, during a busy morning in which he finalized his team's ECHL roster. "I know to a man, and I've met a few of those kids, they wish it all started tomorrow.

"But their bullpen can rest, their big starters can get ready and I think they're going to take the whole thing."

If they do, the coach hopes they savor the special moments that he recalls with such fond memories.

"After we won the Stanley Cup, I got to go home and share it with my mom and dad and the friends I grew up with," Matvichuk said. "To see the look on their faces, that's when you know how special it is. Those kids on the Royals have the entire city and the country excited about baseball, and I'm so happy for them."

• • •

There isn't a bigger Royals fan than Ant-Man star and Kansas City native Paul Rudd.

"When I tell my friends I'm a Royals fan, they're like, 'Oh, so nice,' because everyone loves the team after what they did in the playoffs last year," said Rudd, who every year joins fellow metro-area natives Jason Sudekis, Rob Riggle, David Koechner, and Eric Stonestreet for the annual "Big Slick KC" poker tournament and night at The K to benefit Children's Mercy Hospital.

"With what the Royals did last year, even Cardinals fans like the Royals – well, most of them do. We had Johnny Damon once, and Jermaine Dye once and now we have Eric Hosmer, and we have Mike Moustakas and we have Sal Perez, and I hope we have them for a long time. All the guys who grew up in Kansas City now get to go the stadium, meet the players, throw out a first pitch, take batting practice. I went to the stadium as a kid and it was a thrill but I can't wrap my head around it. There is something about being around professional athletes. I am a fan, I love my team and now I get to be around them and get to know them. Man, it blows my mind."

Rudd attended the postseason in 2014 and said, "There is just a feeling. I feel it, the entire town feels it. I lost my voice at every game. I know for the last several years I had the same hope, 'Okay, the pieces are coming together.' They have made some nice trades, we had high hopes. And I thought this could happen and now it has."

The two most famous lines from last year's playoffs were Jarrod Dyson's "That what speed do" and Rudd's "Party at Mom's house. I got a keg. Five dollar cover."

"Yeah, that kind of developed a life of its own," Rudd said, grinning. "Let's hope we get to do it again this year – and years to come."

• • •

I was born in 1985 and my grandfather had season tickets to the Royals until the 1993 strike. My grandma and grandpa's companies had season tickets and we used them in the 1990s, but when my grandpa died, I pretty much quit going for a year or two. Being at the stadium brought up a lot of emotions about my grandpa. It wasn't that I was not following the team anymore. It was just hard.

Now, on to the good stuff.

I was out of state for most of the playoff run last year. I was in Vegas in February and placed a bet on the 33-1 (odds) Royals at a sports book as a sign of good faith in the rebuilt team. My dad and I went to one regular season game against Tampa Bay, but other than that I was not around to watch the season in person. The playoffs were quickly coming and the excitement was building. I spent all of the Wild Card game riding a bike or on a treadmill at the complex I was staying at that night because that was the only place in Arizona that was showing the Royals game. After the Royals won I went running back to my apartment, whooping and hollering like a mad man. I already knew that the World Series ticket prices were well out of my reach so I had no thoughts of going on a playoff/World Series trip.

Every day I would check the prices of World Series tickets, watching them climb to four digits. I went to every playoff team's site that had a raffle for face value tickets, entering my e-mail and all my relatives' e-mail addresses in hopes we would get the golden ticket to be allowed to only pay hundreds not thousands. The Cards, Royals and a few others all came back without any luck. My hopes looked dashed when my phone showed a red dot – "Congrats you have been selected for the Giants World Series presale!"

I called my mom and she said Dad couldn't go to San Francisco that weekend. I decided to buy the Giants tickets, if nothing else to resell if the Cards and Royals didn't make it. The next day I bought one ticket for Game

3 and one for Game 4 in the bleachers at AT&T Park. A few days later I put in an order for four tickets in St. Louis when the Royals were looking like a lock to clinch. I knew that I was going to see the Royals in the World Series one way or another. The only question was if my dad would get to go or not.

During my down time I designed a shirt for the Negro League Baseball Museum in Kansas City. The museum decided to produce the shirt for the World Series and they were having a viewing party where the shirts would be sold. The prices in KC started to fall, and my mom gave me the green light to buy KC tickets for dad and me if we gave up Christmas and our birthday gifts. We said yes, and I went the next three days looking up flights and tickets.

The original plan was to sell the San Francisco tickets and go to one game in KC with the money from the San Francisco tickets plus a few bucks. As I looked at flights it became very clear that flying to and from KC was going to be very pricy. I then started do some multi-city searches on my Visa rewards card and found I could fly from Arizona to KC, KC to Oakland and Oakland to Arizona cheaper than Arizona to KC. So, it was set: I was going to three games. I cleaned out my rewards points getting one night in a hotel and my cross country travel. The only issue was I would be staying in San Francisco two nights. I spent the next three days making signs to take with me on my travels.

My flight landed in KC and we went directly to the museum to watch Game 1. My shirts were proudly hung in display and we watched the Royals get killed with a group of rowdy fans. The next night was Game 2. Dad and I left early, getting to the stadium a few hours before the gates opened. We watched the ESPN shows that were filming live at the stadium and then we made our way into the stadium with my bag of signs and our museum shirts on. I had just returned from taking pictures of batting practice and flashing my Hunter Pence signs at Hunter Pence, when an usher came to me and told me that they would start doing a game in front of our seats. We asked if we needed to move and the guy replied no do you want to play. I said yes, and waited for the game to start.

The pregame started and they called me over and explained that we would be playing the mountain climber game. They decided to move the game closer to home plate. It was my turn. I was told I would get a prize no matter what, but if I won I would get something better. The screen flashed a Chevy ad and my heart raced. A new car was not the prize, but I thought for a second it might – just might – be my night. The lady before me lost her game and got a GPS system so I was like okay, no matter what, I am getting something good.

The game started and the first item was a frozen pizza I was within a dollar, the second was a couple of pounds of bananas and I was within cents, the last item was a gallon of milk and I basically had won the game at this point. I had tons of money left. I was within cents again. I had won the Jumbotron Game at Game 2 of the World Series. I am thinking "Holy crap, what am I going to get? Tickets to Game 7? Season tickets? A Bo Jackson fishing trip? Whisky with Brett? Maybe $500 bucks to the team store to get World Series stuff, what?" People were like, "Oh my God, no one wins this game," the host was like "that is the best I have ever seen anyone do," and then some intern handed me a generic blue KC shirt left over from the metro whatever giveaway box and nothing else. I was like, is this it? I made my way back to my seat high fiving all the fans and ushers. All the ushers were telling me how I killed it and no one does that good and asking what I won and I held up the $3 shirt.

My dad and I watched the game with a slight lean the entire night because we were located right behind the foul pole down the first base side, which made seeing the pitcher and batter more or less impossible at the same time. As the game went on I flashed my signs as the Royals rallied and as Pence came to the plate. The Royals went on to win the game and we stayed in the parking lot watching the recap show as the crowds moved out.

The day of Game 3, I flew out of KC at 6 a.m. after waking up at 3 a.m. to get from north of St. Joseph (Mo.) to KCI in time for my flight. I packed all of my things into a backpack, leaving my suitcase at my grandparents. My signs were rolled up in a shopping bag. I boarded a flight heading to LAX and then to Oakland and 93-percent of the people on the flight were wearing blue and going nuts. Most had tickets, others were flying out in hopes of scalped tickets. I got to the park and Missouri alum Aaron Crow was out on the warning track. I yelled at the top of my lungs, "M! I! Z!" as he was midway through his wind up to toss the ball back to the infield. He spun around and saw me yelling in my Kansas City road gray uniform, and tossed me a ball.

I sat in the dead center of the bleachers surrounded by Giants fans holding up my signs with every Royals run. Most fans were great, a few were jerks. One guy attacked me and took my Rally Ribs Bib sign after a huge Royals inning. Half the Giants fans cheered half booed him for being a jerk. The Giants fans were all telling me to hold up my sign so they could get a pic of my great Pence signs.

The Royals went on to win and I hung around with a pack of 100-200 chanting KC fans. I made my way to my hotel and met up with a buddy of mine that had just moved to Oakland. We went to a bar called Smugglers Cove, and the doorman saw my KC hat and let me in right away. People up and down the streets were yelling, "Hey, Kansas City!" as I walked by and if I was asked about BBQ once I was asked 50 times which place is best, or if it was really that good.

Well, on to Game 4. I was once again sitting in Giants country but there was a Royals fan and his San Francisco native girlfriend, who was cheering for KC, behind me. The three of us stuck together for the game only to see a Royals loss.

That night I went out with more local friends to the tune of more KC cat calling. I was dropped off at the airport around 1:30 a.m. where I slept on a sofa until my 7 a.m. flight back to Arizona. On my way through the checkpoint I learned a WS mini bat is considered a weapon and had to deal with that.

Charles Sollars
Kansas City, Mo.

• • •

It all started when I was working for a funeral home and got a hearse. I started going to Chiefs games in the 1980s to give them "last rites." Then, I thought why not wear the Pope gear to a Royals game, and the fans liked it so I just kept wearing it. Now, it's just become a part of going to a game, a part of my routine.

I have two girls (Libby, 13 and Abby, 14) and they don't get too embarrassed by Dad. With Pope Francis being in the United States, I'm getting a lot of extra attention from fans. They want my blessing – and I'm happy to give them a Royal blessing. I think people really started to pay attention to me when I caught one of Salvy's home runs. I was sitting in

Bob Danley, who made headlines early in the season when he caught a Salvador Perez home run near the Royals bullpen in left field, dresses as the "Pope" for each home game. He said he would be happy to "bless" any player or fan who seeks his council.

the first row of seats on top of the Royals bullpen, and he hit the ball and I had my glove and caught it. I still haven't been able to get him to sign it, so Salvy, if you are reading these comments, can we get together so you can sign the home run ball I caught?

Bob "The Pope" Danley
Blue Springs, Mo.

• • •

I love my job, and I can't imagine doing anything else. I grew up in a large family and we loved watching Royals games, and now, here I am working at the stadium – greeting everyone who comes in (through the south glass doors of the Home Plate Entrance). We had nine people in our family so we didn't make it to many games in person, but we watched on TV and loved that experience. There is nothing quite as special as sharing a Royals game with members of your family, and now I feel like I have an extended family. I feel like everyone who comes to the game and enters through my doors is a part of my family and I want them to feel welcome and I want them to know that we are thrilled that they are here. This is my third year with the Royals and I can't begin to tell you how much fun I have at each game.

Marge Wolfer
Special Assignments Associate, Greeter at Kauffman Stadium

• • •

I've worked for the Royals 6 ½ years, so I was here through some lean years. We had to deal with a few disgruntled fans back then, but now, everyone is in love with this team. The atmosphere has changed like night and day. And it's easy to see why. This is a young, exciting team and they love the fans as much as the fans love them. People will always ask about my favorite game, and I have to say that I have never been in this stadium when the atmosphere was any better than the 2014 Wild Card game. The World Series games were great, but that Wild Card game was just unbelievable. The fans started standing and cheering early in the game and they didn't stop until Salvy knocked in the winning run in the 12th inning. You hear people talk about Royals magic – well, that's what they're talking about.

Rob Fredenburg
Supervisor Special Assignment Personnel at Kauffman Stadium

• • •

I've worked for the Royals 17 years – I started as a sales intern and I now have the best job in baseball. When I started with the Royals, the Hall of Fame did not exist. We had the area with the Hall of Fame portraits and a few pieces of memorabilia and that was it. Now, we have this wonderful Hall of Fame out in left field that features so many pieces of great memorabilia from throughout the years and all of John Martin's Hall of Fame portraits. I grew up a Royals fan in Tulsa, Okla., and I remember cheering for George, Quiz, Willie, Frank and all the great players from that era. Now, we have our modern-day favorites and I can't wait to see what we place from them and all their success out in the Hall of Fame.

Kurt Nelson
Director of Royals Hall of Fame at
Kauffman Stadium

• • •

I might have to disagree with Kurt (laughing) because I believe I have the best job in baseball. I started out giving a short history lesson before fans visited the Hall of Fame back in 2009. We'd go from the 1800s to the present day and it gave them a taste of what they were going to see and hear (from video messages) in the Hall of Fame. And it all evolved into

Marge Wolfer, right, is the official greeter for anyone who enters Kauffman Stadium through the front glassed doors. 2015 was her third season of making sure every Royals fan feels welcome at The K.

A relatively new icon associated with Royals baseball, "KayCee" dresses in a throwback uniform and hangs a "W" at Kauffman Stadium following every win.

me hanging the 'W' on the Hall of Fame wall after each win. That began in 2014 and has really become a part of the festivities. I talked with Kurt about hanging the 'W' after a win and he said, 'Let's do it.'

I now walk through the stadium wearing my vintage uniforms and visit with fans and pose for photos and I still like to talk about the history of baseball. It's so much fun. I actually made the first 'W,' out of material I had in my garage. Now, we have the big, special 'W' that the players carried around on the field after we won our home playoff games (in 2014), Salvy and Hoz wanted to take a photo with it. That was so special for me. I never dreamed any of this would happen.

KayCee
Former Hall of Fame host who now places "W"
on Hall of Fame following each Royals win

• • •

"This is my 19th year and I never did imagine working during a postseason and World Series. I started out working as a blue shirt – we served as the in-between the ushers and police and I worked three weeks down by the clubhouse. The first person who came through the very first night was George Brett and he asked, 'Is the Brett Suite open?' and I told him, 'It's your suite, of course it's open.' But I learned it wasn't his suite, and he has been through many times and it's always such a pleasure to see George. Bob Gibson came through, Bert Blyleven, rock groups, governors, Whitey Ford came through one night. It's like all my baseball cards have come to life. This was all new to the team last year and now, you never know who you might see on a nightly basis. I've had scouts who come through here and they call me during the middle of the winter to check on me and tell me they are looking forward to seeing me in the press box during the upcoming season.

Mike Witt
Former coach and activities director who is now the director of the press box attendants

• • •

I'm not trying to be the next Vin Scully. I love the game. I just want to have fun. It took a while for the fans in Kansas City to get used to me. They'd ask, 'What's up with that guy? What's his act?' But it's not an act. It's natural. People couldn't understand why I was so happy all the time. Well, I was in the minor leagues 10 years and that's hard. Then, I got to the big leagues and I said I'm not going to let any one person spoil any day I spend in the big leagues and I take that approach to the broadcast booth. I love this team, I love our fans, I love the guys I work with – I love everything about Kansas City.

Rex Hudler
Royals color analyst

• • •

The first time I met the real KayCee he told me that someday I might get his job. My friend's mom made this uniform and KayCee told me I look just like him. My aunt made my 'W' and I like to carry it around. I have fun carrying my 'W' around and having people ask me to take photos with them. I was at all the playoff games and I love the Royals.

Brayden Walker
"Little KayCee," a resident of Lenexa, Kan.

• • •

His uniform was actually his Halloween costume last year. A

Brayden Walker, Lenexa, Kan., is a big hit at Kauffman Stadium as he portrays "Little KayCee," the counterpart to Royals mascot "KayCee," who holds the W sign after each Royals win.

friend mentioned it and my sister-in-law helped with the outfit. He is a hit. The energy around the whole postseason is so amazing. People see him and he will get stuck in a spot and people will take pictures with him for 30 or 40 minutes.

Burke Walker
The father of "Little KayCee"

• • •

(On what the 2015 championship meant to him)

It meant a lot, in terms of as a former player and how when you start playing the game, you put the uniform on to become a champion. To be able to see these guys achieve that goal was pretty special. As a former player, we always want to support the guys of today, and want to let them know we're behind them 100-percent.

(On watching some of the guys he coached in the minors achieve success)

Just to watch Alex (Gordon) go through all the losing seasons here, and all the struggles, as he figured it out at this level. Just to see what he's been able to achieve with all the Gold Gloves. He's the most veteran player on the team. Being able to see those guys from 2006 (who played for White while he was manager of the Royals' Double-A minor league affiliate, including Luke Hochevar) that were young and had dreams of being Major League ballplayers – to see them achieve their dreams, it doesn't get any better than that in baseball.

Frank White
Royals Hall of Famer
8-time Gold Glove Award winner

• • •

(On his experience as a batboy with the 1985 World Series championship team)

It was neat to be there in '85 inside the clubhouse. My first year I started I was 15 years old. What I remember is, heck, back then there were no goggles. There was champagne in my eyes, in the players' eyes. It was old school! It was just a fun, fun time.

You thought it was going to happen every year, and of course it didn't. But here it is 30 years later and I'm still friends with those guys. They've been like big brothers, uncles; I still talk to a lot of them all the time.

(On his experience this year and Kansas City as a sports town)

The fun thing for me is to share this with my son. For him to see the fun, the winning, the celebration, the comeback games. That's just so fun for me to see that for him. It's fun how life and family develop. It's great for the city. Kansas City is such a great baseball town and a sports town. I love it when our teams win.

I expected (the massive crowd at the victory celebration). Kansas City baseball fans are just proud and happy overall. It's a passionate sports town and a baseball town. I think this town is in love with sports and its baseball players. I'm so glad people got to enjoy it again, see it again, and be a part of it.

Chris Browne
Vice President/General Manager
Kansas City T-Bones Baseball Club

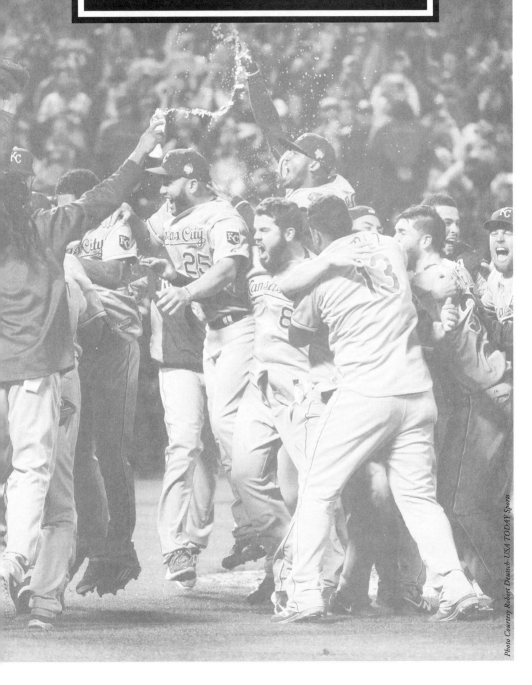

The Gems

Photo Courtesy Robert Deutsch-USA TODAY Sports

CHAPTER 1

2015 American League Divisional Series – Game 4

For more than a year, Kansas City baseball fans have told, and re-told, the story of that amazing 9-8, 12-inning Wild Card game victory over the Oakland A's. Everyone who bleeds Royal blue knows the story by heart; the one where the boys overcome a 7-3 deficit versus Jon Lester – the best postseason pitcher in modern baseball history – to punch their ticket to the American League Divisional Series. It was a road that wouldn't end until Game 7 of the 2014 World Series, and the story gets bigger and better each time it is told.

As crazy as it is to imagine, at this point that comeback almost seems like old hat. That's the type of thing that can happen when a team spends the entire following post-season stringing together one amazing come-from-behind victory after another. That 2014 Wild Card game is no longer unique – it's the first in a series. This season, eight of the Royals' 11 post-season victories included a comeback.

Talk about the Cardiac Kids.

While each story has its own unique pizzazz, its own flair, none was more dramatic than the 9-6 victory in the American League Divisional Series, with the Royals fighting for their baseball lives versus a relentless Houston Astros squad.

With the Astros leading 2-1 in the series, Kansas City's back was squarely against the wall. It was win or go home.

Salvador Perez's early homer gave the Royals a quick lead in the must-win Game 4, but Houston's Carlos Correa hit a solo home run in the third inning that tied things up 2-2. In the fifth, Correa gave the Astros a 3-2 lead with an RBI double and his seventh-inning blast gave Astros fans plenty to cheer about as the lead was pushed to 5-2. Then Colby Rasmus, who hit three homers in the ALDS, connected again and the Royals trailed 6-2 in the seventh.

To put it bluntly, if one were inclined to support the visitors from Kansas City...things looked bleak.

That's when an emotionally-charged Mike Moustakas ran in from third base and said, "I'm not ready to (bleeping) go home!"

Neither were his inspired teammates, who roared to life in the eighth. Three straight singles opened the frame and loaded the bases, and Lorenzo Cain and Eric Hosmer delivered. A pair of RBI singles cut the lead to 6-4.

With the bases still loaded, Kendrys Morales hit a ball up the middle that deflected off reliever Tony Sipp's glove to Correa. The sure-handed shortstop saw it take a strange bounce off his own mitt, and suddenly the score was tied.

Oct 12, 2015; Houston, TX, USA; Kansas City Royals second baseman Ben Zobrist celebrates in the dugout after scoring against the Houston Astros during the eighth inning in Game 4 of the ALDS at Minute Maid Park. The Royals won 9-6, following a stunning comeback that ultimately led to a Game 5 win and a series victory.

The man his teammates call "The Captain," Alex Gordon, then hit a ground ball to second baseman Jose Altuve that drove in yet another run, and the Royals had a 7-6 lead.

But they weren't quite done.

Hosmer, who had struggled offensively in the series, stepped to the plate in the top of the ninth inning and blasted hit a two-run homer to provide Wade Davis, The Terminator himself, with two more runs of insurance.

He didn't need it. He almost never needs it. Davis pitched two innings of shutout relief and just like that the Kansas City Royals were back in business. The series went home to Kansas City, Johnny Cueto threw a historic gem backed by plenty of offensive firepower, and a ticket to the American League Championship Series was punched.

Here, in their words, are manager Ned Yost and Hosmer talking about the improbable win.

"We just want to keep the line moving – I think that's one thing this team does very well, is every game we play we just go out and play our game and stick to our game no matter what the situation is, no matter what happens early on in the game," Hosmer said. "I think we realize that if we just try and focus on playing a full nine innings and continue to stick to our game plan even if we go down to an early lead or have our backs against the wall, we always feel like we're in the game some type of way. And this team has been tested plenty of times with our back against the wall, with our season on the line. I think it's a situation…I don't know I would say if we feel comfortable with it, but we respond well when it comes to that."

When Moustakas came into the dugout following the seventh inning, he and other members of the team were on fire. They knew their season was on the line and something needed to happen.

"You look at that eighth inning and you're down four runs and just realizing as a team, as an offense, everyone's pretty much got one at-bat left, and I just remember everyone saying: 'Just make it count.' Mike was the loudest! But we were all thinking it, saying something. You realize you're down four runs in that situation and no one guy can get us back in the game by himself, so the trust that we all have in each other and just the at-bats that everyone was putting in that eighth inning, you can just tell that that was the mentality was there, it was just fight, fight, fight. Season is on the line.

"And you've got guys like Drew Butera coming off the bench, obviously it's been a little while since his last at-bat and you put him in a pressure situation like that off a closer, to see the pitches he's fouling off and laying off, it's just – it's something that this team really just has, this trust in each other, and it continues to play with no nerves and just let it all out there and let it all happen. And it worked out for us."

There were so many moments in the playoffs when the Royals responded following a mental or physical error by an opponent. Correa's error – which many believed should have been ruled a base hit because of the ball bouncing off Sipp and the turf – paved the way for the first of many Royals opportunistic scoring chances.

"Yeah, that's definitely how I reacted," Hosmer explained. "I was on first base running and really that's when you're talking lucky breaks or good fortune. I think that's one of the first ones we have had all series. You look at some of the stuff that's happened, and some of the balls in the first couple nights we hit that we lost were right at guys, or some guys are just missing pitches and just skying them in the air. Not taking anything away from what Colby has done, but Colby hits the ball yesterday, hits the foul pole and hits the ball the other day and hits the roof up top and just stuff didn't seem like it was really going our way. Until that ball kind of hitting off of Sipp there, and taking a funky hop to Correa, and we're hoping that's the turning point for us as a team. It definitely – if we weren't awake by then – it definitely woke us up."

While his team rallied for the huge come-from-behind win, Yost simply watched the action in the dugout, knowing they would find a way to get the victory.

"The mood in the dugout in the eighth inning was fine," Yost said. "It was fine. The thing about this club is that they don't quit. They don't. And after giving up three runs there in the bottom of the seventh, they came in on fire. Again, like they do. Come on, let's go, good at-bats, let's start it moving. On base, on base, on base, let's go, boys. Let's get it going.

"That was an unbelievable inning. I think we ended up seeing like 53 pitches in the eighth inning. I mean, that just shows you the quality at-bats that we had, at-bat after at-bat after at-bat. So it was a great inning right there. They're a confident group. Six-to-two in the eighth inning doesn't look good, but it doesn't faze them. They come in, they come into that dugout and they're on fire, they're ready to go. Come on, you know, it's like it's a tie ballgame or we're down one. It didn't matter. They just come into that dugout ready go."

Lost in the dramatic hits was the aforementioned walk by Butera, who came in as a defensive replacement after Perez got hit in the mask by a hard foul tip and had to leave the game. His contribution was to walk; to find a way to get on base. He kept the line moving.

"That was a great at-bat right there," Yost said. "Salvy got smoked pretty good in the face, and right in the spot where we kind of guard against, low on the chin. He said he was fine, but that rings your bell a little bit. And then when he got hit by the pitch, I'm like, okay, that's enough beating for one day. We can pinch-run and see if we can't make something happen here, but Drew Butera came in, and not only did he catch great but that was a phenomenal at-bat right there. But you keep looking at this group and our bats were really silent until the eighth inning. but having watched them as much as I've watched them, you know that sooner or later they're going to break out.

"You just know it. You have confidence that sooner or later they're going to put together some hits and they're going to put some runs on the board. And even though we were down four in the eighth inning, I felt real confident that we were going to make a game out of it. I just felt that the bats were going to come alive, and they really did in the eighth inning. I mean really did. Gordo's at-bat was a great at-bat. To get the lead run there with Wade coming in to pitch the eighth and ninth, we felt very, very confident at that point."

CHAPTER 2

The 2015 World Series – Game 1

Eric Hosmer was in need of some redemption.

See, Hosmer is regarded by many as the best defensive first baseman in the American League, if not the entirety of Major League Baseball. He's got soft hands, cat-quick reflexes, and he's not afraid to sacrifice his body for the sake of an out. His infielders love him, because they know all they have to do is get it near him, and it's in the glove. Done deal.

So when the New York Mets' Wilmer Flores chopped a ball down the first base line in the top of the eighth inning, everyone knew it was an out. Everybody. Everybody except the baseball, apparently.

The ball skipped under the glove of a baffled Hosmer and into right field, allowing the Mets to score what appeared to be the likely game-winning run. They had the lead and they had Jeurys Familia ready

Oct 27, 2015; Kansas City, MO, USA; Kansas City Royals former player George Brett throws out the ceremonial first pitch before Game 1 of the 2015 World Series against the New York Mets at Kauffman Stadium.

in the bullpen – the man as close to a National League version of Wade Davis as one could find during the 2015 season.

So Hosmer needed something. He needed a second chance, something to blow the Royals' way and keep the game moving.

Turns out, he needed Alex Gordon.

The man his teammates refer to as "The Captain" turned on a Familia pitch in the bottom of the ninth, sent it into orbit and the game into extra innings with the score tied at 4-4.

Welcome to the World Series.

"I don't have that opportunity if Alex doesn't hit that homer in the bottom of the ninth," Hosmer said. "He's our captain, our leader, he is so important to this team. He put us on his back in the ninth and got the job done."

The game extended another four innings beyond the ninth, entering a three-way tie for the longest ever World Series contest, and fate decided to give Hosmer his chance at redemption. He cashed in on it with a sacrifice fly in the bottom of the 14th inning, driving in the winning run.

After starter Edinson Volquez allowed three runs in six innings, the Royals bullpen allowed just the one unearned run in eight innings. Chris Young, who pitched three scoreless innings in relief for Kansas City, got the win. Bartolo Colon took the loss.

Alcides Escobar, who led the game off with an inside-the-park home run, said Volquez found out before the game that his father had died. He left to be with his family after he was taken out in the sixth inning.

"Man, that is a tough job going out to pitch when you get news like that," Escobar said. (It was later revealed that, in keeping with the wishes of the Volquez family, Edinson was not told until after he exited the game. Which of course does nothing to diminish the tragedy of his loss or the brilliance of his performance.)

Escobar reached first base on an error by third baseman David Wright to open the 14th inning. Ben Zobrist then hit a single that sent Escobar to third base.

Lorenzo Cain was intentionally walked to load the bases, leading to Hosmer's game-winning sacrifice fly.

The Royals jumped in front of the Mets in dramatic fashion in the bottom of the first inning as Escobar crushed flamethrower Matt Harvey's first pitch for an inside-the-park home run. The ball glanced off the leg of center fielder Yoenis Cespedes and darted back along the lower edge of the protective pad on the outfield fence. By the time left fielder Michael Conforto chased it down, Escobar crossed home plate standing up.

"Yeah, you don't see many inside-the-park home runs," Escobar said, grinning. "It has to hit something and bounce away from the outfielders like mine did.

"It was a good way to start the game – and what a crazy game! We go 14 innings, we make some mistakes, we make some big plays and we get great relief pitching.

"No one wanted this to go 14, but it's better to go 14 and win than it is to go 14 and lose."

After pitching no-hit ball for three innings, Volquez gave up runs in the fourth, fifth and sixth innings consecutively. Lucas Duda had an RBI single

Photo Courtesy Jeff Curry-USA TODAY Sports

Oct 27, 2015; Kansas City, MO, USA; Kansas City Royals left fielder Alex Gordon celebrates after hitting a solo home run against the New York Mets in the 9th inning in Game 1 of the 2015 World Series at Kauffman Stadium.

in the fourth, Curtis Granderson homered in the fifth, and Travis D'Arnaud had an RBI sacrifice fly in the sixth.

The Royals tied the game 3-3 in the sixth. Zobrist doubled and Cain singled to right. Hosmer hit a sacrifice to score Zobrist. After Kendrys Morales grounded out, Mike Moustakas delivered a clutch two-out RBI single.

The Mets then reclaimed the lead in the eighth inning when Hosmer misplayed the Flores grounder, allowing the go-ahead run to score.

"It short-hopped me," said Hosmer, who has now won back-to-back-to-back Gold Gloves. "I thought I had it and it skipped off my glove. Thank goodness for Alex's home run. I couldn't live with myself if that cost us the game."

That set the stage for Gordon's ninth-inning homer and Hosmer's dramatic sacrifice fly.

"We just find a way to win big games and pick each other up," Gordon said. "This was a big win. In a series like this, you want to win the first game and we were able to do that tonight."

CHAPTER 3

The 2015 World Series – Game 2

Like any pitcher worth his salt, Johnny Cueto wanted to finish what he started.

The enigmatic starting pitcher, acquired via mid-season trade to be the ace the rotation needed to solidify itself, had been…call it "up and down" since donning the Royal blue in Kansas City.

But there was no question of his mastery over the Mets in Game 2 of the 2015 World Series. This was vintage Johnny Cueto – messing with the timing of hitters, painting the corners, and using a changeup that should probably be illegal to sit down batter after batter. At one point, in fact, he retired 15-straight New York Mets.

So when the ninth inning approached with the Royals maintaining a 4-1 lead, Cueto saw manager Ned Yost eye the abundance of weapons in his bullpen. This was traditionally when he would turn the ball over to the best closer in baseball, Wade Davis, for a 1-2-3 inning and the win. But Cueto wanted that ninth inning. He wanted that 27th out.

He wanted the complete game.

"He came up to me in the middle of the eighth and began to make his case to pitch a complete game," Yost said after Cueto indeed completed a two-hit gem in a 7-1 victory over the Mets at Kauffman Stadium to give the Royals a 2-0 series advantage.

"I told him he'd done his job and with a three-run lead, that's when we bring in Wade (Davis) to get the save. But when we scored the three runs and made it a 7-1 lead, it was easier to agree with him and let him go back out in the ninth."

Cueto nearly danced out to the mound, skipping over the first base line, and worked around a two-out walk to become the first pitcher to toss a two-hit complete game since some guy named Greg Maddux did it back in 1995.

"I felt good in the ninth," Cueto said through interpreter Pedro Grifol, a Royals assistant coach. "I felt good, relaxed, and I knew I had a 7-1 lead. I just had to attack the hitters."

For most of the night, the crowd of 40,410 was chanting "Cueto! Cueto!" when he walked off the mound or had two strikes on a batter.

Oct 28, 2015; Kansas City, MO, USA; Kansas City Royals starting pitcher Johnny Cueto reacts as he puts the final touch on a complete game to defeat the New York Mets in game two of the 2015 World Series at Kauffman Stadium.

Photo Courtesy John Rieger-USA TODAY Sports

"I take a lot of pride in that," Cueto said. "I get a lot of energy from our fans. I feel great when I hear our fans supporting me and backing me in this type of game."

Cueto said he dedicated the game to Edinson Volquez and his family, as his friend and fellow Dominican lost his father before Game 1.

"It was a very sad day for me yesterday," Cueto said. "And there was a lot of focus on my part (today). I dedicated this game to Volquez's dad and the whole family and thank God it turned out this way."

Mets starter Jacob deGrom, who had defeated Los Angeles Dodgers aces Zack Greinke and Clayton Kershaw earlier in the postseason, was touched for four runs in the fifth inning.

After Alex Gordon drew a leadoff walk and Alex Rios singled, American League Championship Series MVP Alcides Escobar singled to center to drive in the first run and tie it 1-1.

Ben Zobrist then grounded out and Lorenzo Cain lined out. Eric Hosmer, for the second night in a row, drove home the eventual game-winning run with a clutch two-out, two-run single that put the Royals ahead 3-1.

The line kept moving. Following a Kendrys Morales single, Mike Moustakas singled to give the Royals a 4-1 lead and a world of confidence.

"The way Johnny was pitching, we felt like all we had to do was give him some kind of a lead and we'd be fine," said Hosmer. "Johnny was great. That's why we made the deal to bring him here – big games like this – and he really came through.

"This win is huge, going into New York with the 2-0 lead. But we can't be satisfied until we win the whole thing. We went to San Francisco last year and had a 2-1 lead and didn't get the job done.

"We haven't forgotten that. That is something we thought about the entire off season, spring training and this season. We aren't going to slow down until we win this."

The Royals added three runs in the bottom of the eighth to give Cueto the cushion he needed to go back out in the ninth. Moustakas singled and Salvador Perez doubled to lead off against Mets reliever Jon Niese. Alex Gordon followed with an RBI double, Paulo Orlando drove in Perez with a sacrifice fly and Escobar tripled to center field to make it 7-1.

CHAPTER 4

All-Access Pass

Have you ever wondered what it would be like to cover a World Series up close and personal?

Picture for a moment the crowd from the 2015 World Series victory celebration, packed onto the field at Kauffman Stadium, crammed into the lobby, and overflowing into the interview room. It's not quite the same as 800,000 people, but it feels like it. Now, find a seat in the interview room, try to snag a player for a one-on-one interview or simply head into the locker room following a game, where the media outnumber the players 25 to 1.

Sound like fun? Well, we've got your back. Here are all the comments from Yost and the key players as the Royals swept aside the Mets in the five-game series, and claimed the crown once more.

Game 1
Royals 5, Mets 4 (14 innings)

Q. When did your starting pitcher Edinson Volquez find out his father died – before or during his start?

NED YOST: I don't have any idea when he found out. You know, we found out about it before the game and the wishes of the family was, you know, let Eddie pitch. So I was kind of keeping my eye, didn't want him to hear about it. I was keeping my eye on him. And he was fine. He didn't know, and I guess after the game is when he found out.

Q. Did you talk to him about it?

NED YOST: I didn't have a chance, the game was going on.

Q. In the game, kind of a crazy game, Alex Gordon's home run put a charge in you guys, and you had to use a lot of guys (out of the bullpen).

NED YOST: You know, you get in that situation with Familia on the mound, you know how good he can be. Gordy hit one about as good as he can hit it to tie the ballgame up, and we just kept battling from that point on.

Q. Did you have a contingency in case perhaps Edinson couldn't pitch?

NED YOST: I did. I talked to Chris Young and told him that if Eddie finds out, you know how tough that can be. I remember Chris just went through it, Moose went through it with his mom. It's a very, very tough thing, especially right before you're about to go out and pitch. It would almost be impossible to do that in Game 1 of the World Series. I told Chris just to be ready in case something happens. And he would have to pick up the slack.

Q. With this team, Edinson pitching, eight innings of relief, one unearned run, Gordon's home run, Hosmer redeeming himself...

NED YOST: It was a great night. Two things you don't want in Game 1 of the World Series: One is to go 14 innings and the other is to lose. To find a way to grind that way out against a great team, both teams were matching pitch for pitch. We had opportunities, they'd make big pitches and get out of innings. But to grind through that game and to win it in the 14th inning was big.

Q. You talk about Chris Young, he's scheduled to start Game 4. How does tonight affect that plan?

NED YOST: It really doesn't. Our plan going into it was we could go 45 to 50 pitches with Chris and bring him back a day early, he'd be fine with that. Once it got to the 50-pitch mark, it was okay, we're going to go all out to win this game, and Chris is going to go as far as he could go. But we ended up winning the ballgame in kind of our threshold there.

Q. Didn't Chris throw 90 miles an hour tonight nine or 10 times? They say first time since 2009.

NED YOST: It's World Series adrenaline, I guess. We felt good about bringing Chris in that game because nothing affects him, nothing.

He's just going to come in and make pitches and hold the fort until we could find a way to win.

Q. Eric Hosmer is a Gold Glover. What did you see on his error?

NED YOST: It was kind of a short hop play. I think he just stepped up to try to catch it on the short hop and he just missed it.

Q. He had several chances at the end and finally made the sacrifice fly.

NED YOST: Yeah, it was big for him. It was kind of redeeming there for him to come up and get the game-winning sacrifice fly for us, right there, it was nice.

Q. I don't remember what inning it was, but Lorenzo Cain, the sacrifice bunt, what was the plan?

NED YOST: No, there was no plan. He was bunting on his own there. We give our guys the freedom to play their style, give them the freedom to bunt. A lot of times we'll put hit and runs on, but I don't think I put four bunt signs on all year. And he just felt like our best chance of winning the ballgame was to get it down, get the runner at third and drive him in from there.

Q. How valuable has it been to have a guy like Chris who can be a swing man, who can start and relieve, do both effectively?

NED YOST: It was a great sign by Dayton Moore late in the spring. He's pitched so well for us all year long in any role we've asked him to do. The thing that's so special to me is the confidence we all have in him. For him to go out and pitch the way that he does under any circumstance has just been a big lift to us all.

Q. Where is Edinson right now, is he still with the team?

NED YOST: No, he's gone home, he left before the game ended.

Q. Do you have any idea what the plan is?

NED YOST: I don't know, I just got in the locker room after 14 innings.

Game 2
Royals 7, Mets 1

Q. How big was it for Johnny Cueto to put up that kind of night coming off his last postseason start (a loss), what he went through?

NED YOST: After the way his last postseason game went... but the game before that (Game 5 of the American League Divisional Series) was exactly like tonight. I mean, his postseason, he's had one bad start and two tremendous starts.

But tonight was everything we expected Johnny to be. He was on the attack. He kept the ball down. He changed speeds. It was just a spectacular performance by him.

Q. What (was it about) about your lineup these last two games against Matt Harvey and then against Jacob deGrom, as you guys get through the third time in the order, that you were able to adjust and pounce on them?

NED YOST: We don't swing and miss. We put the ball in play, and we find ways to just keep putting the ball in play until you find holes. We had an opportunity in the fourth inning and couldn't capitalize on it and the fifth inning we did. We got guys on and guys just kept the line moving, kept finding ways to find holes out there.

Q. Did you get a feeling Johnny was going to be like this tonight?

NED YOST: Yes, yes. I felt Johnny thrives in this environment and he's comfortable in this park. He loves our fans. He feeds off their energy. I just felt very, very strongly that he was going to put up a great performance, and he did.

Q. At what point did you feel a complete game was a possibility for him?

NED YOST: When we scored three runs in the eight, I was going to send Wade Davis in to pitch the ninth. Johnny had done his job at that point. And in a save situation that's Wade's job. Wade was coming in and we scored three. Johnny wanted to go back out. I'm like, 'Look, you've done your job very, very well tonight. And now we're going to let Wade do his. Keep your head in the game because if we score a couple of runs we'll let you go back out,' and we did.

Q. Was Alcides Escobar bunting on his own in the 5th?

NED YOST: Yes.

Q. How do you define "Esky magic," and was that an example of it?

NED YOST: He finds a way to put the ball in play. I knew I didn't put the bunts on him, because I knew he would be bunting on his own, fouled the ball off the first pitch, fouled the ball second pitch. Moose was standing next to me and said, 'Just go ahead and swing away and get a single.' That's exactly what he did. His focus really intensifies during this time. He's a big game player. And he finds ways to be successful in this environment. The biggest environment you can be in. But his focus really, really intensifies. He finds a way to be special during these times.

Q. How much will it help going into New York and having such a well-rested bullpen, especially considering also Chris Young, how much he threw yesterday?

NED YOST: That was key. To score those three runs and let Johnny go back out and finish the game, not use anybody in the pen. Today Wade got loose, Kelvin Herrera got a little loose, but it's not like coming in and pitching an inning. And with the off-day tomorrow, they'll be ready to go for that three-game stretch in New York.

Q. The series isn't over. It's 2-0. Confidence level with how you guys won last night and how you won today, what was the clubhouse like in there?

NED YOST: Our confidence level hasn't changed since the first day of spring training to today. Our confidence has been high all year long. We expected to be here. We expected to compete for a world championship against a tough team. And our confidence hasn't changed from the first day of spring training to this point right now.

Game 3
Mets 9, Royals 3

Q. What did you see from Yordano Ventura? Were you surprised at all to see his velocity that consistently low?

NED YOST: He just wasn't sharp today. Fastball velocity was down. Made a couple mistakes. Made a mistake in the first inning with Wright on a fastball up. The backup slider to Granderson. It was just one of those days where he just wasn't sharp. It was cool. It was cold out there. I don't know if that affected him. He just wasn't sharp.

Q. Besides the cold there wasn't any cause to the velocity?

NED YOST: No.

Q. Nothing mechanical then?

NED YOST: Mechanical? No, I don't think so. He just wasn't sharp. I didn't have any problem with his mechanics. I thought at times he threw good curveballs. I thought he was on line, wasn't flying open with his fastball, just wasn't sharp.

Q. Did you think there were a couple of times he got a little flustered? I'm talking about mostly about not covering first.

NED YOST: Well, yeah, at that point in that game, you could tell he was starting to get a little flustered. Started losing his focus and concentration at that point. That's why we made the move. We wanted to try and hold it right there. And (Danny) Duffy came in and did a great job at that point.

Q. From your vantage point what adjustments did Syndergaard start making at the end of the second and in the middle innings?

NED YOST: No, he just settled in. I don't think he made adjustments. We swing the bat really good against him in the first two innings -- if you're going to get a really good pitcher, you better get him early. And we put some runs on the board against him early. But he settled in. He settled down and started throwing his secondary stuff for strikes and spotting his fastball better.

Q. Medlen can be your long guy sometimes. It looked like tonight you were trying to cobble it together. What went into your thinking with the way you decided to use your pen after Yordano went out so quickly?

NED YOST: Well, we wanted to bring Duffy in to get us through that inning. And then run one-inning stints with (Luke Hochevar) Hoch, (Franklin) Morales, (Ryan) Madson, and (Kelvin) Herrera, hold the fort and see if we could score some runs down the road. But that plan kind of fell by the wayside when Morales came in and ended up getting the bases loaded there, and we were still trying to hold the score at that point at three. So we double-switched there in case we could get out of that early with Herrera, and then send him back out. Of course that didn't work either; Kelvin got his pitch count up and gave up another three runs. And then it was trying to get through it. Medlen can come in today and throw an inning, and still give us two or three innings tomorrow.

Q. What was your view of Granderson's ball back to Morales? What happened on that and how key was that?

NED YOST: Well, that was a key play. That was a big out that we needed to get at that point. We were going to bring in Herrera against Wright no matter what. But we only wanted him to possibly go four outs in that situation, is why we double-switched. Then Kel ended up going five. But it was a ground ball right back to him. And his instincts were right, he was going to turn around and fire to second. And again, I haven't talked to Salvy, but Franklin heard said he heard Salvy say 'home.' So he stopped and turned and it was a mess from that point.

Q. You were up 2-1 in the ALCS and then had a loss in the third game. Do you feel the same, kind of moving on in the series, as you did in the ALCS?

NED YOST: I do. We've all got a lot of confidence in our group. We've got Chris Young going tomorrow and we feel good about that. He's, again, the ultimate competitor. Nothing is going to mess with him, the weather, nothing is going to mess with him. He's going to go out and execute pitches and keep us in the ballgame until we get to our pen. Our pen is in great shape. Matz is going to be tough tomorrow. Got a really, really good curveball and really good fastball. But we're swinging the bats good. So we're all really confident.

Game 4
Royals 5, Mets 3

Q. During the year Wade did not have a multi-inning save for you guys, and it's something you go to a lot in the postseason. I'm curious how you make that transition, and how significant it is to do it?

NED YOST: It depends on his rest. He was the most rested guy we had down there today. We knew if we had a lead in the eighth inning, unless it was multiple-run lead, a three- or four- or five-run lead we were going to go to Wade in that situation. We had Herrera left. We felt all along if we could hold the score at one or two, we could find a way to tie the ballgame up and eventually take the lead, at least that was the hope anyway. So we pinch-hit for C.Y. (Chris Young) after the fourth inning, and then ran our guys out to try to hold the fort there. And everybody did, except for Duff; Conforto ended up hitting a home run off of him. Besides that everybody was great. It just got to that spot where we just felt it gave us the opportunity to win. It was a big game for us to win. To take a 3-1 lead was huge.

Q. Escobar is on 14-game hit streak. Zobrist just hit his eighth double, how important have their contributions been for you guys?

NED YOST: Huge. We're getting a lot of action at the top of the order. We had a lot of tough decisions to make in this game, and one of them was in the fourth inning: Do we pinch-hit Kendrys Morales, with a runner on first base and two outs? And the reason we ended up doing that, is we just scored a run. We wanted to extend the inning if we could. Hopefully he could step up and hit a home run, which he's done more than anyone else in our lineup. But to keep the inning extended for Escobar and Zobrist, who have been the hot hitters to try and get us a lead at that point.

It's key for guys like Lorenzo Cain, who got big hits tonight, Hos, who has been clutch for us with runners in scoring position. It's big.

Q. Could you just talk about the way this game turned out, the way you come back. You're four outs away from losing. You turn it around, you put together the walks, the hits, the errors, just the resiliency about the team, what it says about the team and what it does for this squad?

NED YOST: That's just what our team does. We feel like if we can keep the game close, we're going to find a way to win it. Our bullpen is so dynamic, they give us a chance to win those type of games. And it's a team that just looks for a little crack. If we find a little crack, they're going to make something happen. It's amazing how they do that. And they do that in a number of ways. But the most important thing is they put the ball in play. They make things happen by putting the ball in play, and it's just a phenomenal group.

Q. With the way they did it tonight, what does it mean for this team, the position of this team?

NED YOST: What they did tonight, is what they've been doing the whole playoffs. It's a group of guys that have the utmost confidence in themselves. I don't think at any point these guys thought that they were going to lose tonight. That's just their mindset. That's just the way that they play the game. They're going to go out and they're going to find a way to win.

Q. How do you explain that knack for taking that one inch and then afterward making a giant gap out of it?

NED YOST: I don't know; it's experience. It's character. It's a group of really, really talented players. But a lot of it I think is a mindset. We're in the biggest stage that you can play in front of and these guys are totally confident in their abilities. They're as cool as cucumbers. They never panic because they've been through it before and they know that they're capable of doing it again. And it's just something that they believe in their heart that they can accomplish. And like I said, it's fun to sit there and be the manager of that group. If you handle the pitching right and keep the score here, these guys are going to find a way to come back and score some runs and win this ballgame.

Q. With Rios, what happened on Granderson's fly?

NED YOST: I didn't talk to him, but I think he probably forget how many outs there were.

Q. Should that not happen at this level?

NED YOST: What do you think? (Laughter).

Q. Even though Wade hasn't done these two-inning stints very often, when you have the lead you give him the ball. How good a feeling is that knowing that roll he's on for the last two years he's going to get those outs?

NED YOST: I think he's probably one of the top dominant relievers in all of baseball. Anytime we give him the ball it's just, like, okay, sit back, Wade's in control. So once we got that lead in the eighth inning, we knew what we were going to do. We were going to go straight to Wade and let him close the game out. This time of year it's easier to do what we did tonight, do a six-out save. We did it in Houston and he went through it flawlessly. During the year it's a little bit harder to do because you don't have all these breaks. And you have to get in the mindset, at least I do, anyway, because I'm really, really focused on my pitchers and their usage, and I just always remind myself, Win this game tonight, worry about tomorrow, tomorrow. Don't worry about anything. Wade is going two today, and don't worry about tomorrow. Win this today, and tomorrow will take care of tomorrow. I fully expect Wade to be okay for tomorrow, too.

Q. Did you get a chance to talk to Volquez? How did that go?

NED YOST: I did: He's doing fine. And you'll get a chance to see him here in a little bit. He's excited to be back. He's excited for the opportunity tomorrow and ready to go.

Q. Did you guys talk at all about how that whole thing was handled? Did you have a chance to ask if he was okay?

NED YOST: No, I think we handled it exactly the way his family wanted it handled.

Q. Knowing how close you guys were last year to finishing off everything, and once again being this close this year, how important is it for you guys to put the series away tomorrow?

NED YOST: Again, when you win the first two games at home, going into it your goal coming in here is winning two games here. But you know if you win one here, you've got two games at home, where we're really, really tough. It's going to be important, but it's not going to be the end of the world if we don't. But I think everybody's going to come to the park tomorrow ready to go.

Game 5
Royals 7, Mets 2 (12 innings)

Q. What could you say about Volquez's performance tonight, given everything on his mind?

NED YOST: I thought it was phenomenal. You know, he gave up a home run to Granderson in the first inning, on a changeup that was kind of up in the zone. For him to pitch the way that he pitched, get us through six innings. He had the bases loaded there, but he did what he did so well all year long, is he limited the damage and held them to one run. It was a phenomenal performance by him. You look at our performances, Volky was unbelievable. Herrera with a three-inning stint; he hadn't had one of those all year. And Hoch coming back on his third day for two innings to get the win. And Wade to close it out, our pitching was absolutely unbelievably good.

Q. You look at Salvador Perez's performance, especially with your background as a catcher, and his ability to stay in there despite taking foul tips it seems off of every body part, and still put up those numbers at the plate, helping the tying rally, the go-ahead rally.

NED YOST: He just had a phenomenal series. I think if I had one regret during the whole playoffs was I had to pinch-run for Sal there in that inning. But it opened up the door for us to score five. I really wish that Sal could have been out there to jump in Wade's arm when we got that final out.

Q. Could you talk about your club, the way you endured from last year, and the way you just built into this year in the championship.

NED YOST: You know, last year was such a hard defeat for us in Game 7. And everybody came to Spring Training, I mean, as determined of a group that I've ever seen. That they were going to get back and they were going to finish the deal this time. So from day one there was no doubt in my mind that they would accomplish it. There was no doubt in their mind that they would accomplish it. And the cool thing about this team is everything they set out to accomplish they did. They wanted to win the division; they won it by 11 games. He wanted to win home-field advantage for the playoffs; they did. They wanted to win the World Series; they did. So it's just a special, special group that doesn't come around very often.

Q. For you personally this year after going through losing in seven last year, did this moment of winning it live up to what you thought it would be?

NED YOST: Of course it does. Like I said before the game, this is my eighth World Series; I've lost seven of them. So to be able to win this is very, very special, with this group of guys, with their character, with their heart, with their passion, with the energy that they bring every single day, I mean, they leave everything on the field. It was very, very special to be able to watch these kids grow up from A-ball to Double-A to Triple-A, get to the big leagues, go through their struggles, have their successes, go through their struggles, and develop the point to be world champions is extremely satisfying.

Q. Quite simply, who is Christian Colon? And what were his emotions like coming off the field after the inning in which he gave you guys the World Series?

NED YOST: You can imagine his emotions. He's a guy that last year we took off the World Series roster because he broke his finger, and we didn't think he was throwing well. This year we kept him on, and the reason we kept him on because we felt as a staff, as an organization, that he was a clutch-type player. He's a winner. And you put him in a situation, and he's going to give you everything that he's got. And for him to come through tonight and get the big hit was just – it was special. For Hoch, who's been through Tommy John surgery, been here from the beginning, to be on the mound to get that last out and get the win in Game 5 to make us world champions for me was special.

So you kind of celebrate as a manager all those little achievements that are so special.

Q. What did you say to Dayton Moore when you saw him afterward?

NED YOST: Took me a long time to see him, but I just hugged him. I thought back to when I was managing Milwaukee. Dayton and I were in Atlanta together. A good friend of ours, outfield coach named Jim Beauchamp had passed away from cancer, and both of us were at the funeral. And I was managing in Milwaukee at that time, and Dayton was a new GM in Kansas City. And I saw Dayton, I shook his hand. They were looking for a manager and I said, 'What are you looking for?' And Dayton looked me square in the eye and said, 'I'm looking for somebody just like you.' So for us to be reunited and for us to accomplish this thing together is probably one of the greatest achievements in my life.

Q. How appropriate is it that you won tonight in the fashion in which you won, coming back and grinding it out, and using a guy who hasn't played all month to get the game-winning hit?

NED YOST: You know what, our guys, you never count them out. And Harvey pitched, I mean, unbelievably. He had four pitches that he was throwing for strikes – fastball, great curveball, great slider, great changeup. And for us to go into the ninth inning down two, it never entered my mind that we were not going to score two or three to take the lead at that point. He was just dominating us up until then. But for our guys to go out and find a way to score two at that point, we felt great. And we've said it all along, if we can tie the game, lighten the game, we love our bullpen. We feel like our bullpen is going to be able to hold the fort until we can find a way to score. And Herrera came in and did a superhuman job, three innings. I don't think he's pitched three innings all year. And Hoch, his third straight day, coming to give us two great innings to get us to Wade. It's just a team that never quits, never panics. They just find ways to win baseball games.

Q. How happy are you for a guy like Alex Gordon, who's been here so long, played on some not very good teams, and after almost a decade of being one the game's most underrated players, finally comes through and wins the World Series?

NED YOST: I'm extremely happy for Alex, and I told Hoch both, because both of them were here from the beginning that I'm so happy for those guys. I couldn't have written a better script than Hoch getting a win for this game, after everything he's been through. And for Alex to finally endure everything that he's endured, become Gold Glover, All-Star and to finally win a world championship. I'm extremely proud for both of those guys.

Your Boys in Blue
Game 1
Royals 5, Mets 4 (14 innings)

Alex Gordon

Q. Jeurys Familia had been so good in the postseason, you obviously haven't seen him a bunch. Take us through that at-bat and the thrill of it.

ALEX GORDON: Never saw him before, knew he was really good. Definitely wasn't trying to do that against him. Great sinker, so I wanted to be ready for it. The at-bat before with Salvy, I saw him quick pitch. I wasn't expecting that and I wanted to make sure when I got on the box

I was ready to hit. And he tried to quick pitch me and left the ball right there to hit and with a guy like that you can't miss pitches that he gives you to hit. And that's what happened.

Q. Did Eric say anything to you in the dugout when you came in, like, 'Thanks for getting me off the hook?'

ALEX GORDON: No, absolutely not. We don't do things like that. We pick each other up and we don't hang our heads when stuff like that happens. We understand that baseball is about adversity and overcoming it, and that's what he did. Guys picked him up and eventually he finished the game off with that sac fly. Gold Glove, first baseman, it was a tough hop, but he usually makes that play.

Q. Edinson's father passed away today, and how did you guys all find out? When did you find out? What was it like in the dugout? Ned said family had not wanted Edinson to know.

ALEX GORDON: Most guys didn't know. I found out in I think it was the 14th inning, right before we won the game. I was standing next to Ned and he told me, he said, 'Let's win this game for Volquez,' and explained what happened. I don't think he knew, I don't think most guys knew. In the locker room during the celebration we all talked about it. That's tough. But we're a family, and we rallied around him and picked him up and hopefully everything is okay.

Q. Does anything this team does surprise you now, with the dramatic Postseason victories and the way you always seem to find a way to pull out a big win?

ALEX GORDON: I mean, not really. I'll tell you, we never get frustrated or hang our heads when we're down. We always feel like we can come back and either make it a game or win the game. I think that speaks for our team chemistry that we all pull together and we're all fighting for one thing, and that's to get the W, and hopefully that shows when we go out there and play. I think it does.

Q. I know hitters don't like to be quick pitched. How tough was that for that at-bat?

ALEX GORDON: It's part of the game. A lot of guys do it now. You've just got to understand with the scouting reports you've got to know that a pitcher does that. Luckily I didn't know it, but I saw it with Salvy. And when I got up there I usually like to get loose, but I got ready right away just to make sure. With nobody on, it's part of baseball. So they're trying to get you out any way that they can. We've got a guy that does it, too, with Cueto. It works both ways, and you've just got to be ready for it.

Game 2
Royals 7, Mets 1

Eric Hosmer

Q. How are you guys feeling right now? Cueto, did you see that coming from him? As the thing went on, what were you guys feeling and what was the feeling like in the clubhouse there?

ERIC HOSMER: It's a great feeling. This is why we pitch for home-field advantage so hard. We've got to take care of business here at home. We know we're going to head into a tough environment over there in New York. It was important for us to take these two. As far as Johnny, he was electric tonight. He feeds off this crowd's energy. He wasn't going to go back out there in the 9th unless we got two runs right there. The offense and all the boys in the dugout really wanted to see him go out and finish it. We were glad we put up those two runs so he could go out and finish the job.

Q. With the way this team just keeps winning, keeps the line moving, Gordon's home run yesterday certainly spectacular. Do you just wait for it to happen?

ERIC HOSMER: Yeah, I just think as a team and especially off a guy like deGrom, you know anytime you've got him on the ropes, anytime you have opportunities with guys on base, you've got to make the most out of it. Facing a guy like that you might not get many opportunities like that, so I just think as a team we all realize how important it is and you just really see everybody bear down, put together good at-bats and fight off tough pitchers' pitches, and hope for him to leave it out over the plate so we can do some damage on it.

Q. Your splits batting with nobody on and batting with runners on, your splits are profound. What is it about runners on base that seems to bring out the best in your swing?

ERIC HOSMER: I just try and be aggressive. I just try and get something good early to hit and not miss it. With these guys, with the stuff that they're featuring on the mound, you can't afford to get in a hole with these guys. That's one thing we're consciously trying to do as an offense, get good pitches and not miss them. Because a guy like deGrom, a guy like Harvey, it's too hard to be deep in the count on them, because how effective their pitches are, and how much more effective they make them when they have two strikes.

Q. You talk all the time about having each others' backs and picking each other up. Aside from the obvious with getting the win tonight, how good did you feel for Johnny after what he went through in Toronto to come up with a complete game?

ERIC HOSMER: It felt great. Last night we had to burn the bullpen pretty good. For him to come out and throw a complete game, and really save Herrera, Wade and those guys down there, and getting them two days off heading to New York is huge. That's what an ace does. When you realize that your bullpen is pretty much spent and they're pretty much burned out, he pretty much went out there and put the team on his back and made Wade and Herrera just have a day off and get them those two full days heading into New York.

Q. Were you surprised at all that there wasn't a replay challenge in the fourth inning on that throw?

ERIC HOSMER: Yeah, it's close, you know. But obviously the playoffs you have two. So it's an opportunity where you can maybe try and take a chance and see if it works or not. But at that point in time you realize you've got to score one to win, anyway. As an offense we had to do anything we can to figure out how to get to deGrom. And just glad it worked out for us.

Q. Ned likes to joke about the Esky magic, but when you look at it and see a guy whose strength is not getting on base, as the leadoff hitter for a club in the World Series, what's he doing? What makes this work?

ERIC HOSMER: He's just a spark plug at the top of the lineup. I think everyone knows he goes up there hacking, especially the first time through. And when you look at his at-bats later on in the game, no matter what the situation is, you can just really see him adjust to whatever he needs to do. Whether it's get guys over or guys on third with less than two outs, really just see the adjustment in his swing. You see him trying to shorten up, put the ball in play, if the infield is back. I think he's a really good situational hitter. Obviously the first pitch and the first at-bat of the game is quite impressive, what he's doing with that. But when you look at all of his other at-bats throughout the game he just does a really good job adjusting to the situation.

Q. You make such a big deal of postseason experience, World Series experience. Now up two zip, having gone through what you went through last year, what did you learn from that as this thing now goes back to New York?

ERIC HOSMER: You realize nothing is over. You realize the series is far from over. There's still a lot of work yet to do. Last year we took a 2-1 lead in San Francisco and were feeling pretty good about ourselves, and we had a three-run lead in the next game. You have to realize as a team, as an offense, you've got to keep your foot on the gas and keep pushing because that team with that staff, they have the ability to rail off a couple of good outings in a row, and their offense has the ability to get hot. I think that's one thing we've learned as team is you can't let up at all and you have to keep your foot on the gas.

Johnny Cueto

Q. You are one of the first Dominican pitchers to complete a game in the World Series. In 1981, Fernando Valenzuela was the last Latin pitcher in the Major Leagues to do it. How do you feel after this game?

JOHNNY CUETO: I want to thank God for this opportunity and this outcome and it's a lot of pride being able to do what I did out there today and do it for all of the Dominican.

Q. I know you and Eddie are great friends. How much inspiration did you get yesterday from what he did, and what he was going through with the passing of his father, and what effect did that have on you today getting ready?

JOHNNY CUETO: It was a very sad day for me yesterday. And there was a lot of focus on my part. I dedicated that game to Volquez's dad and the whole family, and thank God it turned out that way.

Q. What's it like when 40,000 people are cheering your name? And how special is it to pitch here at home?

JOHNNY CUETO: A lot of pride, a lot of energy I get from our fans. I feel great when I hear our fans, just supporting me and backing me in these type of situations.

Q. It was pretty clear when they traded for you that they thought you were the last piece to the puzzle here to possibly win a World Series. With that in mind, what does it mean to pitch this well in your first World Series game?

JOHNNY CUETO: That's what they brought me here for was to help win a World Series. And that's what I've worked for and I dedicate this type of outing to my peers, to the organization, to the staff and everyone involved.

Q. Which performance was better, this game or Game 5 of the Division Series?

JOHNNY CUETO: Game 5 of the Division Series, because obviously if we don't win that game, we're not here to experience this.

Q. As it clearly became apparent that your stuff was good tonight, how did your confidence grow to the point that you were trying to push Ned Yost to go back out in the ninth. And then when you had three on the board how did it feel to step back out on the ninth?

JOHNNY CUETO: The longer the game goes the stronger I get. I loosen up, I feel strong. Thank God Ned told me if we score a couple runs in the 8th I would go out. And thank God we were able to do that and I got the opportunity to close this game out.

Q. What was it like going back out there in the ninth inning? It looked like you almost danced out at the dugout and across the line.

JOHNNY CUETO: I felt good. I felt relaxed and I knew I had a 7-1 lead and I had to just attack the hitters.

Q. One of your teammates said they felt really good for you to be able to bounce back from the Toronto game with this performance. How did you feel coming out with this type of performance in this game?

JOHNNY CUETO: It's great to hear that my teammates are backing me and they're thinking the way they're thinking. Never once did I ever think that the whole club wasn't behind me. I've had everyone's support here since I've been here.

Game 3
Mets 9, Royals 3

Yordano Ventura

Q. How aware were you that your velocity was down? And was there a root cause of that?

YORDANO VENTURA: I don't know why. I just noticed when I came in, I saw the radar or looked at some video. I feel great. Felt great out there, I don't know why my velocity was down.

Q. Do you think that affected the results tonight, not being able to get the normal fastball velocity that you normally get?

YORDANO VENTURA: I think it was more of just commanding my pitches, making sure that I was executing my pitches, and I didn't do that tonight. A lot of pitches were just coming back over the middle of the plate, and that's what happens when you leave them up.

Q. What happened on the ground ball to the right side and you didn't cover first?

YORDANO VENTURA: My instinct was to watch the ball right there and kind of just look at Hoz and see if he was going to go home or something, and just got caught watching the play.

Q. Ned mentioned the cold weather, was that an impact at all on you?

YORDANO VENTURA: The cold wasn't a factor at all. I felt great out there. I don't know why the velocity was down. It was just part of it, I guess, but I felt good and the cold wasn't a factor at all.

Q. With the chance to go up 3-0 in the series, how disappointing was it to have this kind of an outing?

YORDANO VENTURA: I don't feel good at all. I had a chance to put the team 3-0 and I didn't do that. But I'll wake up tomorrow ready to cheer on my guys on the team and it's just part of it. We're still up 2-1.

Q. Do you think you guys can finish the series off here or it will go back to Kansas City?

YORDANO VENTURA: I think we can finish it off right here. There's two more games here and I know that we can with get it done here. We play hard and I don't expect it to go back to Kansas City, so we're going to try to finish it off here.

Game 4
Royals 5, Mets 3

Wade Davis and Mike Moustakas

Q. Question for Wade: All year you had pitched one-inning saves, and so to make that transition to multi-inning save, how do you go about doing it? And how does that role change for you coming into the postseason, just physically, mechanically and such?

WADE DAVIS: I don't think it changes much. It's the World Series; you have a lot more adrenaline to wind up and go out there and give everything you've got. A couple more outs really doesn't change anything.

Q. What's it feel like being one win away from winning the World Series, first time for Kansas City in 30 years?

MIKE MOUSTAKAS: It feels great, but we know we've got a tough team we've got to beat again. It's a great ballclub over there. We've got to come back to work tomorrow and find a way to beat these guys again. But it's nice being up 3-1. But again, it's a great ballclub over there that's capable of a lot of stuff.

Q. Mike, so many times you guys have had so many of these rallies, and so many of them also seem to have these quirky moments in them,

like the ball getting through Murphy. Do you guys get an extra surge from that kind of thing or is it all its own making?

MIKE MOUSTAKAS: I think it's all of its own making. We're just trying to put the ball in play. Against a guy like Familia, that guy throws a bowling-ball sinker. And Hoz did a good job of putting the ball in play and make some things happen. It's just kind of how the ball bounced today. It kind of rolled right for us.

Q. After the jam that Wade got out of in Game 6 in Toronto (tying and winning runs on second and third with no outs in the top of the ninth inning), some of your teammates were using words like 'superhuman.' What's it like to watch him to go out there with the lead, knowing those six outs were his to get?

MIKE MOUSTAKAS: Confident. Exciting. One of the best closers in baseball. And he goes out there, he's throwing 98, 99 mph fastballs and 94 and 95 mph cutters. And he's got a breaking ball that's devastating. It's fun to watch, as far as sitting back at third base. It's fun to watch him go to work. It's nice to know that he can come in and close it out for two innings. That's not an easy thing to do, as much as he says it is. It's not easy getting six outs against a great lineup like that. That's some tough stuff to do.

Q. Mike, did anyone in the clubhouse today come in thinking today must be a must-win game, considering a loss would have meant playing the best of three against Harvey, deGrom and Syndergaard in a row?

MIKE MOUSTAKAS: Every game is a must-win game; it's the World Series. You have to win every single game. And like you said, they have four stud pitchers. Matz is a stud, Harvey and deGrom and Syndergaard, those guys are phenomenal pitchers. But it's a big win for us tonight. But, again, every win is big.

Q. That was the first line-drive double play to end the World Series in 50 years. Can you walk us through that, and especially since it had followed that play, that it's tough for you to pick up.

MIKE MOUSTAKAS: Yeah, they moved me from shortstop to third base a long time ago, so it's probably a good thing. But Murphy hit that ball and I didn't make the play. And then Cespedes got a base hit, and at that point we still have all the confidence in the world in Wade. So we're just trying to make a play for him and ended up getting a little fly-ball, line-drive kind of deal and caught it, and looked at first and just tried to make a good play, good throw to Hoz. And I was able to do that and we ended up winning the game.

Q. Wade, you haven't had a lot of innings where you have had a lot of base runners on. When you get those two guys on, do you draw in any recent experiences to take a deep breath and knowing you can get out of this?

WADE DAVIS: Yeah, I think at that point, I hadn't thrown a whole lot of cutters, so I kind of stored that in the back, in case I got in that situation. Fortunately I had a lefty up, where the cutter works a little bit better, and got a little jam line drive, and got lucky on that. I don't think you get too excited in that situation. You really just try to settle down and stay calm.

Edinson Volquez

EDINSON VOLQUEZ: I just want to thank everybody here for their support and worrying about me. And thank you for your support. I really appreciate it.

Q. After what certainly has been a tough week for you, how excited are you to take the mound tomorrow night with a chance to clinch the World Series?

EDINSON VOLQUEZ: Excited. When you win a game like the World Series, it's a dream come true. I think everybody feels the same way. I feel very excited and happy to win the game. We have a chance tomorrow to win the whole thing. We'll see what happens tomorrow.

Q. Since you pitched last, have you done anything baseball related? And if you haven't –

EDINSON VOLQUEZ: I threw a little bit yesterday, back home in the Dominican. I played catch a little bit. And as soon as I got here today, I played catch in the batting cage.

Q. What are your emotions going to be like on the mound tomorrow when you get out there?

EDINSON VOLQUEZ: I think they're going to be very exciting. I just want to thank God for my opportunity tomorrow to be on the mound and show the world what I have to compete with other team and give our a chance our team to win. I'm pretty sure my dad is going to be proud of me when I pitch tomorrow on the mound. We'll see.

Q. It was a very difficult situation when you pitched in Game 1, obviously. Were you okay with the way it was all handled?

EDINSON VOLQUEZ: Yeah, I think that was the best way to tell me because I didn't even know. If they had told me before the game start, if my wife told me before that, I don't even know if I'm going to be able to pitch. She decided to tell me later. And I think that was the right choice because like I say, I don't think I am going to be able to pitch that day if I find out before the game.

Q. Will you honor your father in any way tomorrow? Will you write his name on the uniform?

EDINSON VOLQUEZ: Inside my hat. Put it inside my hat or in my glove. I haven't done it yet, but tomorrow maybe I will.

Q. What can you tell us about your father? What kind of person he was? What kind of influence he had on your life?

EDINSON VOLQUEZ: He was everything for me. He was one of the greatest men. I remember he bought me my first glove and my first spikes, brought me to the field. He knew that's what I want to be, I want to be a baseball player. And he gave me a lot of support and he buy everything for me. He put me in the right way.

Q. Speaking of all your father did for you when you were younger, how much would it mean for you to go out in your first game after this tragedy and to clinch the World Series championship for you?

EDINSON VOLQUEZ: For me I wish he could be here right now and enjoy every game that I pitch. And tomorrow I'm going to be thinking of my mom, and the rest of my family is going to be so happy to see me pitch. My mom told me before I got here: 'Go over there and enjoy the game like you always do and be proud. We are proud of you. And be proud and make people proud, more proud than they are. And your dad passed away,' and she told me, 'He passed away, but he was really happy to see you pitch in the Big Leagues, your dream.' He was real proud.

Q. You've been away from the club but you've seen what happened tonight over and over again this year in Kansas City. What were your emotions as you watched that eighth inning?

EDINSON VOLQUEZ: It was really exciting. I was nervous little bit. Because we were down a couple of runs, and see the ground ball, I can't remember who -- Murphy wasn't able to catch the ball. And I got happy, I'm like, we're going to do it again. We've been doing it all year. I think Johnny (Cueto) was more nervous, more than me a little bit. It's crazy, man. You never know what's going to happen in the ballgame. And I think -- that's how we play. That's the way we play. I think sometimes we got lucky a little bit.

Q. What time did you get to the stadium today?

EDINSON VOLQUEZ: Right before the game start. I drove from the airport and it was a lot of traffic. It was hard to get here. But I finally did and I'm really happy right now because we win.

Q. Just curious, when you did arrive, what kind of reception did you get from your teammates in the dugout? Did anybody say anything that stood out to you?

EDINSON VOLQUEZ: It was unreal. Hosmer and Moustakas and Chris Young, Rios, the whole team, they came out to see me. Dyson and all those guys were like, 'Hey, man, we're excited to see you back on the team.' I never thought I would get so much love from a lot of people, even outside of the clubhouse and out of baseball. And I was like, Wow, I've got a lot of people that really care about what happened to me. And it's a great feeling.

Q. It must have been very hard to decide whether you could come back to pitch. I wonder how you made that decision and when you were able to get to that point?

EDINSON VOLQUEZ: I told them I was going to be ready to play, if they need me. And when I got here today Ned told me that, 'Hey, are you able to pitch?' I said, 'Yeah, that's why I'm here. I want to pitch. I want to make people proud.' That's what I love, period. That's the only thing I know. And I was like, I thought about it in the dugout. And Johnny goes,

like, 'Hey, you going to pitch tomorrow?' And I say, 'You want pitch?'
He said, 'No. That's your game now, and make your dad proud.' That's
what he told me. I said, 'All right. I'm going to take the ball tomorrow.
It's going to be exciting.'

Game 5
Royals 7, Mets 2 (12 innings)

Salvador Perez

Q. Just take us through your emotions. Let's start with the ninth inning, you're down 2-0. Go through the ninth inning and talk about the confidence of this team?

SALVADOR PEREZ: You guys know what we do all season. We never quit.
We never put our heads down. We never think about, okay, the game is
over, no. We always compete to the last out. And that's what we do tonight.

Harvey threw a tremendous game today. He didn't miss too many pitches.
But in the ninth inning Lorenzo Cain took a good at-bat, good walk.
Hosmer follows with a double, and after that it was history.

Q. Compare, I guess, the on-top-of-the-world feeling that you have with that World Series MVP trophy now, with last year making the last out in Game 7 at home.

SALVADOR PEREZ: I already forget about last year. So I just enjoy the
moment now. In 2015 Kansas City is No. 1. Who cares about what
happened last year?

Q. In the last month you've taken foul balls off the face, off the hand, off the collarbone. What is it that you do to enable you to put the pain aside and keep on playing?

SALVADOR PEREZ: What I always say, I think it's part of my job. Take a
foul ball, wild pitch. And it had to get out of the game, because I feel like
I'm not going to do nothing for my team to win. So I just need a couple
of seconds. I know the pitch didn't go nowhere but to calm down a little
bit. And the good thing we learn, we'll be in another World Series. So

I just like to help my team to win, to play hard, and that's what we do.

Q. Did any of those injuries almost force you out of the game?

SALVADOR PEREZ: No, the one that hit in my face, that was a big one. I feel a little dizzy, but the good thing, I stayed in the game.

Q. You signed with these guys when you were 16 years old. How do you put into words your growth with them in the time since and the organization's growth in the time since?

SALVADOR PEREZ: It's unbelievable. I always say we feel like a family here. We've got the same group, almost the same group when I play my first year in 2007 in Arizona, the Rookie League. It's amazing to now win a World Series and see the same guys with you. It is exciting.

Acknowledgements

When I was asked to write a book on the Kansas City Royals' remarkable run during the 2014 and 2015 seasons, I couldn't say yes fast enough. I am one of seven metro area media types who have been lucky enough to cover all four World Series and every exciting postseason run. I honestly thought that last year's World Series appearance might be the last we would witness for a while – then, this young, energetic and inspired Royals team burst out of spring training with one goal – to return to the World Series and come back to Kansas City as world champions. This fascinating season provided so many wonderful stories, both on and off the field. We will never forget the love of the game displayed by Salvador Perez, the professional approach taken by Alex Gordon both in the locker room and on the field, the maturation of Lorenzo Cain, Eric Hosmer and Mike Moustakas, the brilliance of Wade Davis and the steady, guiding hand of manager Ned Yost – the right man to lead a team that believes in the importance of sharing its success with its fans. This is my eighth book, and in many ways, my most satisfying because I've never been around a group of players who made it so easy to support. They play the game the way it should be played – with passion, grit and determination. When they get down late in a game they don't panic, they just keep the line moving. And that line moved all the way to World Series championship.

I would be remiss if I didn't thank some very special people. First and foremost, this book is dedicated to Stacy, Zach, Sean and Grandma Bubbles. Next, my friend, mentor and publisher Bob Snodgrass. If he were a baseball player, he would be a Royal because his passion for his profession is parallel to what the Royals bring to the plate every time they step on the field. My editor Aaron Cedeno is simply a joy to work with. He and Bob were the 1-2 punch that kept me going. My wife Stacy is my rock, my mom Joyce is the biggest Royals fan I know and Dr. Curt Cavanaugh performed a delicate surgical procedure on my partially paralyzed mini-wiener dog Marley that allowed her to return home and sit in my lap as I finished the book. Marilee Merithew, your transcription was top notch; and of course I want to offer a special thanks to the Zobrist family and everyone who offered up personal stories and photos for this book. The title of this book, "From the Guys Who Were There," is not an empty one. From the start, we wanted this to be different. We wanted it to reflect the spirit of the players and fans – the beating heart of Kansas City itself. And we could not have done it without your help. Thank you.

To the players, staff, and front office of the Kansas City Royals all I can say is – it's your world, thanks for letting us live in it.

Bill Althaus

About the Author

Bill Althaus is an award-winning sportswriter and columnist from *The Examiner* in Eastern Jackson County, Mo. He has been a member of *The Examiner* staff the past 33 years and has been honored by United Press International, the Associated Press, and the Missouri Broadcasters Association for his work on the *Sonic Locker Room* radio program. The Simone Awards Committee named him the first print winner of the Gordon Docking Award for Sports Excellence in 2006, and he won the Morris Excellence in Journalism Award the following year. In 2015, he was named the top Class II columnist by the Missouri Press Association – his seventh individual honor from the committee.

The Independence, Mo. Native lives with his wife, Stacy, in Grain Valley, Mo. They have two sons, Zach and Sean. This is Bill's eighth book. He has covered the Kansas City Royals since 1976 and was the team's beat writer from 1982 to 2003.

Visit www.ascendbooks.com for more great titles!